Advance Praise for
The Mentoring Difference

"Janet Birgenheier ends her fascinating, unique book with 'connecting is a perpetual human need…' This book is profound in its simplicity and openness. Mentoring, a major component of personal and professional development, is often overlooked and mostly 'accomplished' by corporations assigning someone to be someone else's mentor. This approach has a long history of failure, and Janet shows why. Mentoring cannot just 'happen.' It is organic in origination and personal in practice, its foundation based on trust, safety, vulnerability, and competence.

"The book brings the reader up close and personal with the journeys of people through an important period in their lives. They share intimate details of how mentors impacted and helped them uncover attributes and aspirations that many thought to be impossible. People's stories transcend a 'learning process' and expose more than any teacher or facilitator could ever explain. You will relate to these stories and come away reflecting on how you might want a mentor and be a mentor. Life is, indeed, about connecting. Here's an opportunity to see how connecting can be so important."

- Glenn Schenenga, performance and career coach,
organizational development professional

"My bookshelves are sagging under partially read, abandoned books. Not *The Mentoring Difference: Stories to Inspire Your Career Transformation*. I read it in a day. I bet you do too. Throughout I kept reflecting back, with new insights and a much deeper appreciation, on all those who helped me navigate three careers – tenured professor, business owner/ consultant and corporate executive. In her stories Janet Birgenheier reminds us of our responsibility to ensure those in our sphere of influence achieve their inherent potential and provides tangible ways to do so. A must read for both mentors and those looking to transform their lives."

- Emil Bohn, Ph.D., full-time granddad &
mentor to granddaughter, Mary

"Janet Birgenheier's rich and insightful book brings together 10 examples of organic mentoring relationships. Real-life stories trace the development and impact of mentoring on lives and careers. She identifies seven common themes in the mentoring process that enable a mentee to connect, learn and evolve in a mentoring relationship. Most importantly, Janet describes how to cultivate a 'readiness mindset' so that we are primed to receive the great gift of mentoring and prepared to nurture it."

- Ann Rolfe, founder of Mentoring Works and
author of *Mentoring Mindset, Skills and Tools*

"If you are looking to move forward in your career, change career, or simply seek a warm, charming and uplifting set of compelling stories about a diverse group of real people, this is the book for you! Janet Birgenheier's writing is heart-felt and provides meaningful insights into values and dreams that drive all of us. Every page demonstrates a clear passion for helping people find purpose in both their professional and personal lives. Like me, you'll likely emerge from *The Mentoring Difference: Stories to Inspire Your Career Transformation* with a renewed excitement for life."

- Alan Schnur, Ph.D., The Schnur Group

"*The Mentoring Difference* reminds us about the power of sharing our stories. While it is true that a good mentor helps you become a better professional, these stories show us that a *great* mentor helps you become a better person. These heartwarming and poignant stories illustrate the importance of mentorship because no matter the industry, human connection is what gives us the most fulfillment in a career. I highly recommend this book as it will inspire you to seek a great mentor in your field who can help you become your best self, not only at work, but in all areas of your life. And after that, you will want to become a mentor too!"

- Hayden Lee, MCC, master certified executive life & leadership coach

"Focusing only on what's 'urgent,' as too many of us do, we lose sight of what's merely 'important.' Reading *The Mentoring Difference* was, for me, a great opportunity to step back and reflect on the important mentors who have meant so much to me. And to elevate on my priority list my own commitment to being a better mentor."

- Jeff Grimshaw, author of *Leadership without Excuses* and *Five Frequencies: Leadership Signals that Turn Culture into Competitive Advantage*

JANET BIRGENHEIER

THE
MENTORING
DIFFERENCE

Stories to Inspire Your Career
Transformation

Birgenheier, Janet
*The Mentoring Difference: Stories to Inspire
Your Career Transformation*

ISBN 9798653016196

Independently published
Printed in the USA

Design by Damonza.com
Author photograph by Gary Seeman

*For Fermo Gianesello, who made
all the difference to me*

Contents

INTRODUCTION

Barry Brandenburg was planning to mentor his son, Bennett, through Washington State's law clerk program. Growing up, Bennett had viewed his dad, a criminal defense attorney, as a sophisticated arguer. Just before formal mentoring began, Bennett discovered a surprising, new dimension of Barry. He witnessed his dad wisely counsel a jailed female client on a drug possession charge about her life choices. Leaving the jail, Bennett got in his car and cried. He was overwhelmed by the empathic, caring side of the man he thought he knew so well. And, it was a paradigm shift for Bennett to realize that law is about people.

Donna Sinclair was at a low place emotionally on her first day of class. Then she heard Dr. Bill Lang lecture about Pacific Northwest history. He was talking about Native and non-Native concepts of time. Gazing out the window, she started having epiphanies about history and the human experience. Until then, she had never heard how historians pull together past remnants into a coherent narrative. It was a watershed moment that led to her calling after Bill and Dr. Jacqueline Peterson started mentoring her.

Kevin Jordan's mentor, Peter Richter, would quiz him after meetings. He would ask Kevin questions like: "What did you see happen? What was the body language? What didn't happen?

Why do you think that person is happy?" Peter would also draw Kevin's attention to the "meeting within the meeting." He was challenging Kevin to analyze the instant messaging exchanges during meetings. These Socratic conversations opened Kevin's eyes to complex and subtle organizational dynamics.

Liz Williams was taking a clowning class with her mentor, Jean Westcott, to learn handling authority figures with a light touch in their organization development work. On a rainy, windy morning before class, Liz was carrying their lunch to the car. Suddenly she dropped the bag of food and drinks. With her injured hands, Liz struggled to pick up everything the wind was blowing around. Jean was leaning on the car laughing. Then, Liz started laughing so hard she fell onto the wet pavement. It was the last time that dropping things embarrassed Liz. Jean had empowered her to be her natural, playful self and keep mishaps at work in perspective.

These were transformative career and life lessons for Bennett, Donna, Kevin, and Liz. Their mentors had shaped their perspective through example, teaching, and attitude. In this book, you will read their full stories along with those of six additional mentees – including me. In every case, wise, caring, accomplished mentors guided the mentees' career transformations.

Applying the Stories to Your Career

If you've longed for such a person to make a difference in your own career journey, this book is for you. And, it is about much more than admiring wonderful, wise mentors who influenced mentees' career and life journeys – decades ago in most cases. Taken together, the 10 inspiring stories offer deeply relevant, timely themes for those of you seeking a meaningful career. The stories demonstrate the powerful difference that a mentor can make in guiding your transformation. And, the mentees who shared their stories offer personal insights into how you can best receive a mentor and nurture the relationship.

Planning, Researching, and Writing the Book

The experience of my own beloved mentor, Fermo Gianesello, was the catalyst for the book. I met him when I was 25. He shaped me in important ways, became a dear friend, and we had a 20-year relationship until he died. My husband, Dr. Gary Seeman, had heard my story of Fermo many times, although they had never met. One summer evening in 2019, Gary and I were strolling across the scenic Washington State University Vancouver campus. I had just mentioned my mentor, and Gary said, "You really should write your story. People would find it inspiring."

I responded, "Of course! That makes perfect sense!" After a few more steps, I added enthusiastically, "And, I bet there are lots of other mentor stories out there just waiting to be told. I could write a book about mentoring, and each chapter could be a different person's story of how their mentor shaped them." I knew at that moment that I would capture some compelling stories. And, I vowed to dedicate the book to Fermo.

I reached out to my network of colleagues and friends to describe my idea and gather stories. Within a half hour, I heard from Liz Williams in the San Francisco Bay Area. She was eager to share her story. Soon I had commitments to contribute stories from a diverse and successful group of professionals.

The stories of five female and five male mentees cover a varied range of fields. Industrial marketing communication, criminal defense and personal injury law, alternative primary education, university French education, Jungian-oriented psychotherapy, the business side of health care, executive and leadership coaching, public history, holistic spiritual guidance, organizational consulting, and restaurant entrepreneurship are represented. Despite such diversity, the mentoring process across the stories reveals common themes, which are covered in chapters 2 and 13.

It was fascinating to interview the mentees and preserve their stories. They recounted their experiences in stream-of-consciousness fashion, pulling in vivid memories over many years like colorful threads woven into a rich tapestry. I got to help them relive their past. In the process, several of the mentees shared new insights they gained from reflecting on their careers many years later. I became the steward of precious stories, and it was an honor.

As a career coach, I hope the stories will inspire you to embrace mentoring and fulfill your calling. Here's to your future!

Janet Birgenheier
Ridgefield, Washington
www.meaningfulwork.coach

CHAPTER 1

EMBRACING THE POWER
OF MENTORING

*"Mentors offer us something that we need in
the moment – something we have been missing
without realizing we were missing it."*

*– Chuck Bender,
Jungian-oriented psychotherapist*

∽

IT'S DIFFICULT TO overstate the power that mentors have to influence our careers. They are very special people who appear in our lives – perhaps when we don't even know we need them. Mentors guide and shape us in ways that we can't imagine when we meet them. They help us gain our professional footing and build confidence. And, their impact is typically not limited to our work. When we engage with mentors, we learn so much more than how to transform our careers. We also integrate precious lessons about ourselves and life – often developing lasting friendships in the process.

Unfortunately, many of us move through our lives without having had such a mentor. I see the effects of this in my work as a career coach. After retiring from a long career in corporate America, I launched my coaching practice to guide my clients in realizing their visions for meaningful work. I help them identify their calling based on personal values, passions, and natural talents. (And, I typically recommend that my clients be open to career mentors in addition to my services. I say more about that under "Differentiating Career Coaching from Career Mentoring" below.)

In my coaching work, I have encountered clients in every age group and career stage who have struggled to find their way into a truly meaningful work life. Many are not excited about – or may even detest – their current job. They might have experimented with a variety of jobs and remain uncertain about where to focus. When they come to me, most of my clients haven't yet identified a career with purpose. Or, if they've targeted such a career, they may not know how to gain a solid footing. Others have gotten stuck at a dead end and need to start over, but they face daunting obstacles.

Multiple factors can contribute to these circumstances. They may have been trying to live up to the career expectations of others – parents, siblings, colleagues. Some haven't ever experienced a person close to them really "getting" them, seeing their talents, and believing in them, so they struggle with self-doubt or low self-esteem. Younger clients may not have lived enough life yet to know themselves, what they want, or to have encountered door-opening opportunities. Others have been unable to complete their education. There have also been clients who told me they got "the wrong" degree, one that hasn't led to a fulfilling, viable career. For some clients, priorities have shifted due to life events, forcing them to make new choices.

A significant missing element in many of these cases has been a career mentor to guide and inspire them in a promising field.

Defining Mentoring

According to the University of Cambridge website, "Mentoring is a system of semi-structured guidance whereby one person shares... knowledge, skills, and experience to assist others to progress in their lives and career... Mentoring is more than 'giving advice,' or passing on... experience. It's about motivating and empowering the other person to identify... issues and goals, and helping... find ways of resolving (the issues) or reaching (the goals)."[1] In practice, this means that mentors serve as guides, advisors, experts, teachers, guardians, and friends. Above all, they are role models.

Mentors are invaluable in shaping our careers. They can make *all the difference* between a lackluster career and a meaningful, successful one. I believe this based on my own experience of having had a powerful mentor in the early years of my corporate career. I tell my story in chapter 3. In chapters 4 through 12, I tell the stories of nine additional professionals who transformed their careers and lives under the guidance of their mentors.

---

1   "What Is Mentoring?" University of Cambridge. Accessed February 12, 2020.
https://www.ppd.admin.cam.ac.uk/professional-development/mentoring-university-cambridge/what-mentoring.

Differentiating Career Coaching from Career Mentoring

There is an important distinction between *career coaching* and *career mentoring*, although people often use the terms interchangeably. As a *career coach*, I am a thought partner who guides my clients to examine their personal values, passions, and natural talents in order to explore career options and identify a meaningful career. Then we develop the strategies and tactics to embark on a career transformation. During the process, I help my clients address the challenges that were blocking their career fulfillment.

But, many clients also need specific guidance in the technical aspects of their targeted field. So, I advise them to be open to receiving a *career mentor* – someone with extensive experience and expertise – a subject matter expert – in that field. I consciously use the word "receive" because I believe that mentors appear when we're ready to receive them. The 10 mentor stories in this book bear that out. Chapter 13 addresses the timing element, and chapter 14 describes the readiness mindset.

Experiencing the Mentor-Mentee Relationship

Jungian-oriented psychotherapist Chuck Bender characterized the essence of the mentoring relationship as "a meeting of consciousness" between mentor and mentee. He elaborated on the nature of this powerful relationship from his personal experiences in both roles. "A deep recognition takes place between two people who share a passion for something. There's a two-way resonance."

And, in sharing a passion, mentors guide their mentees

to learn what they don't yet know, according to Chuck. "Mentors offer us something that we need in the moment – something we have been missing without realizing we were missing it," he observed. Chuck likened this process to awakening a dry riverbed and getting the water flowing in the mentee.

He described a brief mentor relationship he had with the late Dr. Donald Sandner, a Jungian analyst best known for his book, *Navaho Symbols of Healing: a Jungian Exploration of Ritual, Image, and Medicine.* In 1996, Chuck saw Dr. Sandner speak at a "Friends of Jung" event in Portland, Oregon, and read the book. A single line in Dr. Sandner's book about the motif of death and rebirth jumped out at Chuck. It answered an important question with which Chuck had been wrestling. He called this "a mentoring moment." So, he yearned to learn more from Dr. Sandner to inform his own mentoring of a men's group that was exploring life and death. Chuck had identified a shared passion with the Jungian analyst.

He later wrote a letter requesting the opportunity to work with Dr. Sandner. Chuck was delighted when Dr. Sandner responded by proposing a trip to spend time with him and his fellow mentors of the men's group. So, Chuck hosted a weekend event at his home in Southwest Washington. The group studied "a major myth" that exemplified the death and rebirth theme. He recalled, "I remember dropping him off at the airport afterwards, and Don said that he had a great time, that it was really fun. Then, he invited us to come down to his beach house in San Francisco in September 1997. I really felt a kinship with him."

But, the San Francisco meeting never took place. In April 1997, Chuck received the shocking news that Dr. Sandner had suddenly died of a heart attack on March 30. Chuck's mentoring experience had been compressed, yet it had also been extremely powerful. Dr. Sandner's legacy enriched Chuck's work mentoring other men at full day gatherings and weekend retreats in the woods for many years to come.

Chuck reflected further on what's behind the deep recognition that takes place between mentee and mentor. "The mentee recognizes the mentor's depth of understanding. The mentor, in turn, recognizes the mentee's potential. As they work together, they grow into a shared recognition of these qualities, and they are both called to bring into being what didn't exist before they came together," he observed.

He added that this fosters a relationship of deep affection in which the mentor puts the mentee's professional and personal growth needs first. It creates a foundation of mutual respect. The mentor, like a good parent, protects the mentee while nurturing growth toward achieving full potential.

Dr. Gary Seeman, a clinical psychologist who also works with a Jungian orientation, added his perspective on the importance of the mentor containing the mentee's transformational process. He commented, "The mentor provides a safe place where transformation can occur undisturbed and be clearly witnessed. The mentor protects the mentee from outside interference, while encouraging the mentee's curiosity, skill-building, and confidence. Their implicitly shared affinity for the work and mutual trust support enthusiasm and experimentation."

Embracing the Organic Process

Mentoring relationships develop organically. They emerge and evolve when the right conditions come together for mentee and mentor. The key is being open to mentoring with intention – whether for a relatively brief period, like Chuck's experience, or more typically for a longer-term relationship with one or more mentors.

This book offers four steps to embrace the organic mentoring process:

1. Learn the power of mentoring through the 10 stories of mentors who dramatically shaped their mentees (introduced in chapter 2 and featured in chapters 3 - 12).

2. Discover the common themes across these stories (introduced in chapter 2 and featured in chapter 13).

3. Cultivate a mindset of readiness to receive a mentor (chapter 14).

4. Nurture the mentoring relationship (chapter 14).

TRACING THE ORIGINS
OF MENTORING

The word "mentor" originated in the Greek myth, *The Odyssey*. In his old age, Mentor, the son of Alcimus, befriended Odysseus. Then, before Odysseus left for the Trojan War, he asked Mentor to watch over his son, Telemachus, and his palace. The goddess Athena disguised herself as Mentor to hide from the suitors of Telemachus' mother, Penelope. In her role as Mentor, Athena guided Telemachus to "stand up against the suitors and go abroad to find out what happened to his father. When Odysseus returned to Ithaca, Athena appeared briefly in the form of Mentor again at Odysseus' palace."[2]

The term has been adopted to mean a person who "imparts wisdom to and shares knowledge with a less-experienced colleague." In the first recorded modern usage, Mentor appeared in Les Aventures de Telemaque, published in 1699 by Francois Fenelon, as the book's main character.[3]

---

2   "Mentor (*Odyssey*)," Wikipedia. Accessed February 12, 2020. https://en.wikipedia.org/wiki/Mentor_(Odyssey).

3   "Mentor (*Odyssey*)." Accessed February 12, 2020.

Gregory Nagy, a classics professor at Harvard University, provided further insight into the role of mentors. He explained that Athena's intention was to impart "menos," which means "heroic strength," into Telemachus. Nagy described this as mental strength – a "surge of power you feel in being able to put things into action."[4]

Mentorship systems have thrived in multiple religious traditions and cultures. Elders in Christianity and Rabbinical Judaism have guided their disciples for centuries. In Hinduism and Buddhism, disciples have learned from gurus. And, apprenticeship was practiced in the medieval guild system.[5]

---

4   B.R.J. O'Donnell, "The Odyssey's Millennia-Old Model of Mentorship." *The Atlantic*. Accessed February 12, 2020.
https://www.theatlantic.com/business/archive/2017/10/the-odyssey-mentorship/542676/.

5   "Mentorship," Wikipedia. Accessed February 12, 2020.
https://en.wikipedia.org/wiki/Mentorship.

Chapter 2

Savoring Mentor Stories

"It has been said that next to hunger and thirst,
our most basic human need is for storytelling."

– Khalil Gibran[6]

✎

THE STORIES THAT follow in the next 10 chapters are as varied as they are inspiring. Yet, common themes unite them. The average age across all the mentees was 27 when mentors first appeared in our lives. And now, decades later in most cases, we have reflected back on our mentoring experiences and what our beloved mentors have meant to us.

A single, long-term, mentee-mentor relationship is the focus in most of the stories. In a few cases, the mentees recounted their experiences with more than one mentor. Some mentors were the managers of their mentees. In other instances, the mentors were family members.

---

6 "26 Quotes About Storytelling," Drew Gneiser. Accessed February 18, 2020. http://www.drewgneiser.com/26-quotes-about-storytelling/.

My story took place in Connecticut. The other nine stories were set in Florida; Southwest Washington; Portland, Oregon; the San Francisco Bay Area; the Silicon Valley; Victoria, British Columbia; and Zarka, Jordan.

Some well-known mentors show up in three of the stories. Rebecca Keith's mentor's mentor was Mario Montessori, son of education method founder, Maria Montessori (chapter 5). Russell Delman's mentor was Moshe Feldenkrais, founder of the Feldenkrais Method of body movement awareness (chapter 10). And, Liz Williams' mentor's mentors were author Ken Blanchard, best known for *The One Minute Manager*, and cross-cultural anthropologist Angeles Arrien (chapter 11).

Overcoming Challenges and Transforming through Mentoring

In every case, the mentees were struggling with significant challenges that their mentors helped them overcome. Wife and mother Therese Brooks desired greater fulfillment through self-understanding. Kevin Jordan had stopped growing and found himself at a professional crossroad. Liz Williams had no idea how to launch a third career after sustaining back and hand injuries. Rebecca Keith was a young wife and mother striving to help support her family. Donna Sinclair, Bennett Brandenburg, John Greene, Russell Delman, and I needed grounding and guidance in emerging careers. And, as one of 10 kids living with his family in a Palestinian camp, Issa Abudakar faced the uphill challenge of getting a university education in his home country or migrating to the United States to pursue his dreams.

Each story demonstrates how the mentee made a gradual,

life-changing career transformation through the guidance and inspiration of one or more mentors.

I advanced over the years from a corporate novice to a seasoned organizational change professional – both as an internal leader and an external consultant. From a psychology graduate with an unclear career path, Bennett Brandenburg blossomed into a full partner in his father's criminal defense and personal injury law firm. Rebecca Keith, a struggling wife and mother of two toddlers, discovered Montessori education. She ultimately founded and heads a school with three campuses and leads a Montessori training center. John Greene advanced from an entry-level French professor at the University of Victoria to the department chair and an administrative leader of the institution. Therese Brooks transformed from a wife and mother yearning for intellectual stimulation into a Jungian-oriented psychotherapist specializing in women's life transitions.

Kevin Jordan took a strategic gamble, fundamentally altered his career arc, and transformed his professional trajectory into a fulfilling leadership and organization development role at Kaiser Permanente. Then he launched his own executive, leadership, and career transformation coaching practice. Donna Sinclair, a waitress and single mother of three young children, became a Ph.D. level public historian, author, professor, and politician. Russell Delman, who started out teaching yoga and meditation, founded and leads an international school of awareness, *The Embodied Life*. Liz Williams managed her hand disability, which truncated a second career, and evolved into an accomplished organizational consultant, trainer, and facilitator. Issa Abudakar completed his education in the United States and became a successful restaurant entrepreneur.

Being Attracted by Mentors' Attributes

The mentees described the attributes that attracted them to their mentors and made for successful relationships. Collectively, these attributes explain the power of mentoring.

Liz Williams and Donna Sinclair both emphasized how their mentors recognized innate talent that was worthy of development. Although Liz and Donna didn't see their own talent, their mentors developed them by opening doors and providing opportunities.

Rebecca Keith commented that she was drawn to her mentor because of the woman's energy, excitement, and enthusiasm for Montessori education. "It made me want to follow, watch, emulate her, and listen to her advice," Rebecca explained.

Bennett Brandenburg characterized his mentor as "willing to sacrifice himself to bring out my strengths and pass on a role and wisdom because he has run the race." Bennett added, "I wanted to follow him closely — like the concept from ancient Jewish tradition of young students following their rabbis so closely that they were covered in their rabbis' dust."

Russell Delman's experience was powerful because of his mentor's open-mindedness and sense of wonder. To express these qualities, Russell recited a few lines from Mary Oliver's poem, *Mysteries, Yes*. "Let me keep my distance, always, from those who think they have the answers. Let me keep company always with those who say 'Look!' and laugh in astonishment, and bow their heads."[7]

---

7   "Mary Oliver Quotes," Good Reads. Accessed February 18, 2020. https://www.goodreads.com/quotes/1200218-mysteries-yes-truly-we-live-with-mysteries-too-marvelous-to.

Kevin Jordan depicted the multiple dimensions of his mentor. "He challenged my thinking and helped me see what I hadn't been seeing, pushing me deeper into uncomfortable spaces and forcing me to grow. But, he also listened empathically, blended strategic advice and thoughtful questions, told the truth, and it was all predicated on trust," Kevin explained.

John Greene described his mentor as someone he "respected and admired, who provided guidance in a way that I could receive without resisting it." He contrasted his mentor with his father, from whom it had been much harder to accept advice because of their relationship.

Issa Abudakar's main mentors were his father and brother. He recalled, "They steered me in the right direction, listened to me with open minds, but also weren't afraid to tell me the truth." Issa explained that their mission was to "improve my life, so they never sugar-coated things or told me what I wanted to hear. They helped me develop my strengths, improve on my weaknesses, and they kept me grounded in a professional direction."

Therese Brooks' mentors inspired her because they helped her "expand my capacity for understanding and relating to others and for seeing myself more clearly."

The magic in my own relationship was rooted in my mentor's underlying loving nature. It was so easy to learn from him how to become a corporate professional because he believed in me and cared about my well-being beyond our roles as manager and staff member.

The love between mentor and mentee is evident in all 10 stories. In the words of Tibetan Buddhist teacher, Namgyal Rinpoche, who died in 2003, "The ideal relationship to the

Teacher is based on friendship, not on awe."[8] He advised students to "focus on the heart to heart relationship to the outer teacher rather than an intellectual one."[9]

Looking for the Themes

Taken as a whole, the stories reveal seven themes, which are grouped under three aspects of the mentoring process:

Connecting with the Mentor

> Being ready at the right time to receive a mentor
> Enjoying shared passion and personal chemistry

Learning from the Mentor

> Learning from role models – professionally and personally
> Feeling safe to show vulnerability
> Accepting challenges to learn what we didn't know we needed

Evolving into Independence from the Mentor

> Experiencing the relationship evolve organically
> Leaving the nest

I invite you to savor the stories, look for the themes in each, and reflect on their meaning for you. Chapter 13 elaborates on the themes with representative examples from the stories.

---

8   Rab Wilkie & David Barry, eds., *Tales of Awakening: Travels, Teachings, and Transcendence with Namgyal Rinpoche (1931 – 2003)* (Fairhaven Lantern Media, 2012), 93.

9   Wilkie & Barry, *Tales of Awakening*, 54.

CHAPTER 3

GETTING MENTORED FOR MY SUCCESS

"My lessons from Fermo extended well beyond our work and the fun we had doing it. He was a man of impeccable integrity… always a consummate gentleman who demonstrated a fatherly protection of me."

᠀

I T WAS LATE 1973, and I was fresh out of college with a Bachelor of Arts in English from the University of California at Davis. My dream was to snag a job where I could write and edit every day. Seeking a change of scene, I moved from Santa Rosa, California, to charming Fairfield County, Connecticut. I had a stint as a cub reporter for the *Bridgeport Post*, but I wanted to earn enough to share rent with roommates. So, I ventured into corporate America by taking an editorial assistant position at Electrolux's Stamford headquarters. In those years, it was challenging for college educated women to land entry-level corporate jobs other than as administrative assistants. My Electrolux position was half administrative assistant and half editorial assistant. In the editorial role, I wrote the company's sales newsletter. It was my introduction to business communication.

After a few years pumping out articles featuring vacuum cleaner sales, I was ready for a more challenging and compelling role. So, in 1976, I responded to an ad in the *Westport News* for an editorial assistant at the Industrial Valve and Instrument (IVI) Division headquarters of Dresser Industries in Stratford. Little did I know that I was about to meet a man who would be so much more than my manager. He would mentor me, and his guidance, influence, and long-term friendship would greatly shape my corporate career and life perspective. Most important of all, the experience would be an example of Namgyal Rinpoche's "heart to heart relationship to the outer teacher" noted in chapter 2.

He was Fermo Gianesello, IVI's Manager of Advertising and Sales Promotion. I don't remember much about the actual interview, but he offered me the position within a few days. The product lines – valves and pressure/temperature instruments used in various types of plants – didn't exactly inspire me. But, I embraced the opportunity to learn business-to-business marketing communication in a technical industry.

As with Electrolux, my initial role was a blend of administrative and editorial duties. So, I typed memos that Fermo dictated into a recorder and processed stacks of vendor invoices. But, very early into the job, he began guiding me to execute his vision of creating two publications from scratch – a newsletter for manufacturer's reps and a magazine for distributors.

That captured my interest. The prospect of planning, launching, and regularly turning out these new publications was thrilling. He later confided in me that my hybrid administrative/editorial assistant position was the initial step toward his real objective – getting budget approval for a full-time publications role. Fermo knew how to creatively navigate corporate obstacles. And, he achieved his objective when he was allowed to promote me to publications editor after a year. I became a full-time writer/editor with my own office, and Fermo hired a full-time administrative assistant. My days of typing memos and processing invoices were over.

Constantly Learning

I never stopped learning new skills from Fermo during the five years that he mentored me. From the moment we began planning the two publications, he took me under his wing. Fermo started teaching me about the audiences, how these publications would enhance the manufacturer's rep and distributor relationships, and why that mattered. With his deep background in industrial advertising and sales promotion, he educated me about layout and design, photography, type-setting/mechanical preparation (the precursor to electronic files), printing, and distribution.

The practical, hands-on lessons were in the fine details. Fermo demonstrated how to use a pica ruler and write captions that would fit the designated space beneath a photo. I learned to avoid placing photos of people with their faces turned toward the outside edge of a page. He trained me in proof-reading galleys of typeset copy. He pointed out the importance of eliminating awkward "widows" (one or two stray words that carry over to the next line). He showed me how to work with a freelance designer who turned my typeset copy into mechanicals. And, we took field trips to printers so I could see how mechanicals were transformed into the printed page.

After the newsletter and magazine were firmly established and another staff member started helping me write articles, my role expanded. Fermo instructed me in writing copy for product brochures. That's where I learned the difference between product features, functions, and benefits – a distinction that I still see missing in many product descriptions today.

Product training seminars for distributors were my next frontier. Fermo understood how such training would enhance distributor sales, so he initiated this new program and gave me an important role. It was my introduction to corporate training, and I learned the process from scratch – presentation objectives, content design and development, slide and handout production, collaboration with product managers who delivered the technical presentations, and program evaluation. I also learned the logistics of planning and conducting training events at offsite venues. This early experience was seminal. It prepared me well to develop two innovative training programs for financial services organizations later in my career.

Building Confidence in a Male World

At some point, Fermo saw that I was ready to tackle a new skill that would prove invaluable throughout my professional life – speaking in front of audiences. He asked me to deliver a presentation on a new communication initiative at a national meeting of the sales organization. At age 26, I was terrified of speaking in front of 100 men I had never met, and many of them were decades older than me. But, fortunately, I was on the agenda for day three. So, I had time to get acquainted with them over cocktails and dinner before stepping onto the stage. I overcame my fear when I started perceiving the guys as approachable colleagues. This helped me to relax and focus on rehearsing my presentation, which I delivered successfully with confidence. Fermo knew I was ready, but I had to experience it for myself.

Everywhere that I went in IVI, I was surrounded by men in professional roles and women who supported them – typing their memos, making their travel arrangements, taking their phone messages on pink note paper, and booking their appointments. My male colleagues were not used to seeing a woman in a non-support role. My office was across the hall from a conference room. One day, an out of town male visitor poked his head in my door to ask if I would make coffee for the meeting. I asserted politely but firmly that coffee was not in my job description, and I explained how he could get his coffee request fulfilled. The interaction infuriated me, and I later shared the incident with Fermo. He smiled and said he was proud of me for how I handled myself. My emerging confidence was growing under his guidance.

Distributor councils created another opportunity to hold my own in this male universe. Fermo collaborated with the sales manager to plan and conduct annual meetings of the top distributors. The meetings took place offsite over several days and covered a wide range of topics. Fermo placed me on the agenda so I could get to know my distributor magazine audience better, solicit feedback on my publication, and collaborate with them on planning future content. He made it clear that I was there to learn and gather input, not to take minutes. One of my fondest memories was interacting with these distributors, who consistently praised my magazine and pointed to the positive impact it was having on their business. Over time, we developed mutual appreciation and comradeship through these annual events. This was also an early experience in meeting facilitation – a skill I would continue to refine over the years.

I learned subtle but significant things from Fermo about interacting with male colleagues. One day early in my IVI career, his boss, the vice president of sales and marketing, called us down to his office to discuss something. I started marching down the hall with Fermo toward the stairs when he abruptly stopped me and said, "Hey, you don't have to move so fast. Glen doesn't expect us to arrive in a split second. It's OK to walk at a normal pace." It was an important lesson in self-regulation and poise. We shared a good chuckle over my youthful exuberance.

Assertion with confidence was an important skill that I picked up from observing Fermo's interactions with our technical colleagues. Our department was responsible for writing all the IVI advertising and sales promotion materials. And, we relied on product managers and engineers for technical reviews, which were intended to ensure accuracy. End of story, right? Not exactly. When reviewing our copy, these colleagues sometimes tried to impose their own writing style. Our drafts might come back with edits that introduced run-on sentences, confusing language, inconsistencies, or other readability issues. Fermo was a master at asserting boundaries on style and creativity. He set an example that I followed for standing my ground when technical reviewers trespassed into our territory. This assertiveness skill would be relevant in a wide range of professional interactions throughout my career.

Finding Joy at Work

But, our day to day office life wasn't all work and no play. Fermo knew how to have fun and infuse joy into the workplace. Being Italian-American, great food was his passion, which he eagerly shared with his staff. He regularly took our department out to lunch at a favorite, local Italian restaurant, where he entertained us with stories about his mother's traditional multi-course, Christmas Eve dinners. While we lunched on fresh pasta in savory sauces, we heard about his lively experiences working for Pitney Bowes and other corporate tales from his past. Fermo's zest for life and grasp of details emerged in his storytelling. Over time, we got to know some of his colorful, former colleagues through these stories.

Traveling for business with Fermo was its own adventure. We schlepped through power plants and climbed onto heavy equipment in the hot, humid South, toting cameras and briefcases. But, it was fun because he made it fun. He always found humor in everyday situations. Once when dragging ourselves through the New Orleans airport at an uncivilized hour, I struggled to maneuver a large, art portfolio case onto an escalator. He observed my struggle and burst into one of his hearty laughs as he lent a hand. Then, I started laughing. It energized me for the drive to our hotel at the late hour.

Alexandria, Louisiana, was the site of the IVI valve plant, and we made trips there several times a year. We couldn't visit the place without a meal at the best, local fine dining establishment, complete with white linen tablecloths. Before my first Alexandria trip with Fermo, he prepared me by describing his favorite menu item – Oysters Bienville. This traditional New Orleans divine concoction was created by baking oysters in shrimp sauce. I was not disappointed the first time I experienced the crusty, mouthwatering bit of heaven on Earth. From then on, our Alexandria agenda always included Oysters Bienville.

Such pleasurable experiences were lessons in the power of bonding with colleagues to enhance collaborative, professional relationships. I later applied this important dimension of work in many career situations.

Witnessing Character Strength

Learning from Fermo extended well beyond our work and the fun we had doing it. He was a man of impeccable integrity. Even though we spent a good deal of time together in the office and on business trips, he was always a consummate gentleman who demonstrated a fatherly protection of me. Fermo became my standard for how men should treat women in business. And, he instilled in me the importance of integrity.

Fermo had many things going for him. He was joyful and fun-loving, never turning down the opportunity to tell a story or a joke with a twinkle in his eye and a contagious laugh. His creativity was wide ranging as a writer, illustrator, photographer, and painter. He once brought into the office a peacock painting that he had just finished. My jaw dropped in admiration of the fine brush strokes and vibrant colors in the tail feathers. He also had a sharp head for business. Fermo could plan and execute a sales promotion strategy with the best of them. And, he worked hard with seemingly unlimited energy, often saying that "coffee and a cigarette" were his lunch break.

But, Fermo was so much more than his lively personality, talent, and energy. He had genuine character strength. I witnessed him endure an unfathomable personal tragedy, pull his family together, and ultimately rise above intense emotional pain. He never lost his enthusiasm for life and his loving nature.

Fermo genuinely cared about his staff as human beings. During one of the annual distributor council meetings, I was suddenly struck with a severe, abdominal pain in my left side and could barely move. He dropped everything, drove me to the hospital, and stayed with me until the doctors determined that I was suffering from a spastic colon, which gradually subsided over the next day.

Another time, I called into work to say that I was staying home because I had hardly slept the previous night after a deeply troubling episode in my personal life. He sensed that I needed emotional support. We lived in the same town, so he said he was picking me up at my home and driving me to work. We had previously scheduled a trip that day to an IVI plant an hour north of the office, and he insisted on keeping our appointment. I got two important things from him that day – his wise perspective on my personal angst and a lesson in fulfilling important work commitments, even after a sleepless night.

He modelled how to be caring, resilient, strong, and to always look for the good in people and in life. I've carried these lessons with me to this day and still occasionally ask myself, "What would Fermo do in this situation?" It's the ultimate gift a mentor can pass on.

Savoring a Long Relationship

I eventually reached a point in my five years working with Fermo when I needed to find a different job. My first husband and I had moved farther away from my office, so my commute had become unsustainable. I landed a marketing officer position for Citicorp (now Citigroup) in Harrison, New York. The role was a great next step in my career evolution. I was going to apply everything Fermo had taught me to internal marketing communications for the asset-based finance subsidiary of this global financial institution.

When I sat in Fermo's office and anxiously broke the news to him, he took it graciously and congratulated me. Then he wiped a tear from his eye. I knew that I was wrapping up an important chapter in my professional life.

But, by then we were friends, and we stayed in touch over the next 15 years. I hosted him and his wife, Carole, for dinner at my home in New Rochelle, New York. After I moved back to northern California, we got together a few times during his business trips out West. Of course, each visit was a delightful opportunity to catch up on our lives.

We also occasionally talked on the phone. During one such conversation in 1996, I shared the joyful news about my engagement to Gary Seeman and described our plans for a June 1997 wedding in California to be followed in October by a Long Island family gathering.

Fermo said he would happily attend the events on both coasts. I was especially looking forward to finally introducing him to Gary, with whom I had shared much about my mentor and friend. But, that would never happen. I received a phone call in June 1996 that he had died suddenly of a heart attack at age 67. Our 20-year relationship had ended.

Living the Legacy

He's not here anymore, so I can't call him, text him, email him, share photos with him on Facebook, or see his smiling face in person. But, his spirit lives on in my memory, and this much I know for sure. My life would have been very different if I had not answered that ad in the *Westport News* in 1976.

The skills and lessons I learned from Fermo prepared me well for a long, successful career in business communication, corporate training, and change management.

About a month after starting my Citicorp job, an incident occurred that deepened my gratitude for Fermo and drove me to assert myself in a disturbing situation. I had drafted an article about a Citicorp-financed industry and shared it with my new manager. His reaction shocked me. He became enraged, attacked my work, and accused me of incompetence. I was shaken to the core. Had I made a huge mistake taking this job? How could I have left a mentor whose respect and admiration I had earned to receive such appalling treatment in my new role?

I mulled over writing a memo to document the incident for two vice presidents – my new manager's boss and the human resources executive. But, first I called Fermo to get his input. The plan was risky. I had only worked in this job a short time, and I would be going over my manager's head, yet his behavior had been entirely unacceptable. Fermo agreed that I needed to take action, advised me to calm down, sleep on my plan, and write the memo the next day. So, I wrote and delivered the memo.

The two vice presidents discussed the situation with me, and in short order, they demoted my manager to an individual contributor. They assigned another colleague and me to a different manager, who was well regarded. They also assured me that they valued me and looked forward to my future contributions. I had mustered the courage to enlist their support because I had learned from Fermo to be confident in my talent and assert myself when necessary.

I did make important contributions to Citicorp and ultimately advanced to vice president. My promotion was in recognition of an innovative product knowledge conference program that I created and led for four years. The program launched in the U.S. and ran three times a year. It rapidly gained international visibility as bankers around the world requested attendance. In the last year I led the program, my team and I conducted conferences in London and Santa Margherita, Italy. The program had become so highly valued that the executive for whom I developed it introduced me to the CEO, John Reed.

Building on My Citicorp Success

I also worked for Charles Schwab, Kaiser Permanente, and Symantec in management roles.

At Schwab, I created another innovative program – this time in stock option education. I developed it for employees of the brokerage firm's corporate clients. As with the Citicorp conference, this program grew rapidly through popular demand. It helped differentiate Schwab as a stock option industry leader and was described in the firm's annual report. The program also provided a speaking opportunity for me at an industry conference, and I was featured in a promotional videotape.

The highlight of my Kaiser tenure was communicating with management about national bargaining in 2005. Kaiser and union leaders in the Labor Management Partnership undertook a bargaining process every five years to negotiate a new agreement. I attended the sessions over six months to keep management informed about the process and outcomes. It was a unique opportunity to interact with a wide array of leaders in a highly visible role.

As an external consultant, I built communication and training programs for numerous other Fortune 500 companies – working for Kwasha Lipton, Towers Perrin and Watson Wyatt (before the Towers Watson merger), and PricewaterhouseCoopers. I also ran my own change management consulting practice. In that role, I especially enjoyed communicating a business model transformation to Cardinal Health employees and traveling to England and Switzerland.

Continuing to Evolve

Beyond skill building, my horizons expanded because Fermo exposed me to new life experiences. I became more joyful, curious, and adventurous. Perhaps that contributed to my decision to earn a Master of Science in organization development in my mid-50s. Most important of all, the courage and character strength that he modeled continued bolstering me for ongoing challenges over the years. Fermo had evolved into a father figure. I could not have had a better mentor at exactly the right time in my life.

Thank you, Fermo.

RECONNECTING WITH FERMO
THROUGH HIS DAUGHTER

Mentors with whom we deeply bonded before they died can live on in unexpected ways. While writing my story of Fermo, I recalled how he used to talk about his three kids so lovingly. That brought to mind thoughts of his daughter, Amy Gianesello-Violette. She was a teenager when I worked with her dad and met her. I became curious about Amy. Does she still live in Connecticut? How is she? What is her life like now?

So, I found Amy on Facebook and scrolled far down her timeline. Then, my heart nearly stopped. I came upon a photo that she had posted of Fermo on Father's Day 2014. It was a professional portrait of him in a business suit. Time raced backward. He looked exactly the way I remembered him when we met 43 years ago. It felt like he was right there in my office as I was writing.

I wanted to share my story draft with Amy. But, I didn't know the best way to contact her. Eventually, I found her place of employment through LinkedIn and mailed a hard copy of the draft with a cover letter to her at work. That was on September 11, 2019.

I wasn't sure if I'd hear back from her. Would she even remember me? Then, on October 3, 2019, an email popped up in my inbox from Amy. She communicated that she didn't want to let another day go by without thanking me for the "eloquent" story I had written about her dad. Yes, she remembered me, and yes, she was enthusiastic about the book!

Then came the punchline in her email message. Amy explained that she hadn't been in the office when my package arrived because her landscape design work had kept her in the field. But, her boss had brought the envelope to her. She opened it on September 23, 2019, which would have been Fermo's 91st birthday. What a meaningful way to reconnect with him!

CHAPTER 4

FINDING HIMSELF THROUGH LAW

"My dad taught me the law is about people, not strict guidelines. It was a paradigm shift to understand that I could be a person with my clients. Now I see my job as being a person first and a lawyer second."

❧

W HEN BENNETT BRANDENBURG entered George Fox University in 2008 in Newberg, Oregon, to study psychology, he never imagined that he'd end up practicing law. His dad, Barry, had started his own law firm in Vancouver, Washington, in 1993. His specialties were criminal defense and personal injury plaintiff cases. So, Barry's son grew up surrounded by law.

Bennett recalled, "I thought of law as an avenue for people to receive justice, but what I cared about was being with people, which is why I was fascinated with psychology. As an introvert, I'm not the most outgoing guy, but I love serving people and having social interactions. Psychology was a way to understand people, and I thought I could go into private practice working with people one on one, so I majored in psychology and minored in Spanish."

But, as Bennett approached graduation with magna cum laude honors in spring 2012, the reality dawned on him that having a psychology private practice would mean completing a master's degree or possibly even a Ph.D. He wasn't sure he wanted to do that. Around the same time, he began to discern the connection between psychology and law. He reminisced, "I realized that my dad's profession was about the issues that people face in their lives. The field of law is full of psychology because it's about people, who have stories that are far greater than what's happened to them, the mistakes they've made, who their parents said they were or weren't. So, I saw the bridge from psychology to law."

He also grasped the dark side of law and psychology. Citing the prevalence of substance abuse among attorneys due to high job stress, Bennett observed, "Unfortunately, we can wear our clients' stories sometimes in unhealthy ways." He pointed out that psychologists can also be susceptible to high stress from treating clients "who have significant trauma in their life."

Pivoting to Law

Nevertheless, Bennett felt called to law in order to serve people and started seriously considering law school for the first time. "I hadn't thought about law school in the past because my mom, Letha, always said she thought I was too nice to be a lawyer. I believed that you had to be mean to be a lawyer. She witnessed how much stress the profession had caused my dad, and she didn't want me to experience that," he explained.

But ironically, his mom mentioned an intriguing program offered by the Washington State Bar Association. The Admission to Practice Rule 6 (APR 6) Law Clerk Program is a four-year alternative to law school that costs $1,500 per year. It involves working and studying under a mentor lawyer or judge to gain theoretical, academic, and practical experience in preparation for the bar exam. APR 6 provides the resources to find all the same books as law school and requires periodic tests administered by the designated mentor. That said, program participants must access the books themselves and create their own syllabus. Those who successfully pass the bar exam after completing APR 6 become licensed to practice law and avoid costly tuition.

When Bennett was considering the merits of law school compared to the APR 6 program, Barry shared his perspective. His dad had been a non-traditional student, having attended Lewis and Clark Law School over four years at night while working in the insurance field. "My dad told me I wouldn't miss anything by not attending law school because it trains people to think like lawyers, but not how to be lawyers. The APR 6 program covers the same books combined with hands-on learning 30 hours a week in a law firm. He saw that as the way for me to learn the practice of law and how to deal with people," Bennett recalled.

Taking the Road Less Traveled

So, he enrolled in APR 6 working at Brandenburg Law Firm with his dad as his professor and mentor and planned to start the program in October 2012. But, before launching into APR 6, he began working in his dad's office the previous spring to get his feet wet. He explained, "I had to learn the ropes starting at the front desk answering the phones. I didn't know anything about how to talk to people."

That year, Bennett was among 62 APR 6 students in contrast to 1,680 students who were attending one of Washington's three law schools. He was clearly taking the road less traveled. And, success was by no means guaranteed. At the time he entered the program, APR 6 had a track record of fewer than 20 percent of students completing the program over the previous five years. However, according to the Washington State Bar Association, of those who completed, an average of 85 percent passed the bar exam.[10] According to Bennett, the pass rate for traditional law school students was around 72 percent.

He cited the benefits of the road he chose. "When I was in the program, my friends in law school said I was a lot farther ahead of them taking the same subjects. They had no context for the subject matter. For them, it was books. For me, it was reality because I was studying and applying the learning at the same time. And, many law school graduates end up spending another $3,000 to $4,000 for a bar exam prep course because they didn't get that in school. Then, during their first few years of practicing law, they get their butt kicked working in a prosecutor's office where the real learning happens."

At first, Bennett felt that he wasn't in law school like his friends. "Then, I realized that I actually was in a different form of law school and that I was doing the harder thing than my friends. And, I've had many people tell me that," he reflected.

---

10   Laura McVicker, "Like Father, Like Son at Local Law Firm," *The Columbian*. Accessed March 8, 2020.
https://www.columbian.com/news/2012/aug/31/brandenburg-law-apprentice-ship-Vancouver/.

Commanding a Presence

Having Barry as his mentor wasn't new to Bennett. "We've been buddies my whole life. Growing up, Dad and I did everything together – Eagle Scouts, snowboarding, golf, hunting. He was my baseball and soccer coach. He's always been my mentor, and I've looked up to him," Bennett explained.

He reminisced about contrasting experiences of his dad as a boy. "At home, dad would hang around in an old fraternity sweatshirt, and we would argue and butt heads about stuff. But, then he'd drive me to the courthouse. I'd come into his world and watch the way he commanded a presence when he'd walk into a courtroom to make an argument. I remember thinking I didn't know who he was then, that he was so cool. Although I didn't necessarily want to be a lawyer at that time, I still wanted to be cool like my dad."

Learning to Be a Person

To Bennett, being like Barry eventually came to mean being "enthusiastic about caring." He told a story that dramatically illustrated his dad's caring quality. "One day before I started the APR 6 program, I accompanied my dad to the jail to see a young, female client in a drug possession case. He was meeting with her about a guilty plea in exchange for reduced time. I observed him counsel her about her life choices. She was considering going back to stripping to make ends meet because she had to care for a young child. He was counseling her on how her life was so much bigger than her drug addiction and challenging her about how that might play out."

He continued, "In the past, I had this image of my dad as difficult, and he would frustrate me. I didn't realize that he was training me to be a sophisticated arguer because he was a lawyer. I learned techniques to argue with him, and we butted heads a lot because neither of us would concede to anything. So, I had never seen this counselor side of him before that day at the jail. I remember getting back in my car and crying. I just broke down feeling overwhelmed with what I had just watched my dad do. When I saw him later, I hugged him and said I was sorry because I didn't know that about him. It was a 'please forgive me' moment, like the prodigal son. It was very humbling to acknowledge who he really is."

Bennett described his dad as "more extroverted than me, able to very accurately see the heart of the situation, and get along with everyone." In the jail, he witnessed Barry acting as "a father figure to this woman who might have never had that kind of relationship."

And, Bennett learned a transformational lesson from the experience. "My dad taught me the law is about people, not strict guidelines. It was a paradigm shift to understand that I could be a person with my clients. Now I see my job as being a person first and a lawyer second. It takes a long time to learn how to be a person. I'm still trying to figure that out. But, my dad has modeled it well," he observed.

Going Way Beyond the Textbooks

When father and son began their mentor-mentee journey together, Barry commented that this work would be the most significant thing he'd ever do in his law practice. But, he had his moments of self-doubt. He would sometimes say to Bennett that he wasn't a professor and that he barely got through law school. And, he felt pressure from his colleagues to do right by his son when they would say to Barry, "We'll find out what kind of professor you are!" Yet, Bennett acknowledged, "Dad would try his best. At times, I felt he didn't put as much effort into the program as I did. But, the irony is that so few people finish this program because the work is on you, the mentee, to do everything. The mentor guides you along."

And, Bennett received a wealth of guidance from Barry that went way beyond the textbooks. He pored over his books in evenings, and during the day, he was immersed in the real world of a mature law practice. Bennett learned first-hand the complexity of representing clients accused of crimes and witnessed his father be a superb role model. "I've watched my dad become superhuman in these really difficult, criminal cases, especially when it's intense subject matter, and we must interview victims of abuse, violence, etc. I've observed him not behave the way we think of lawyers – as being rude. He's acted like a mediator who says to the people he interviews, 'I understand what you're going through.'"

Bennett learned to keep the big picture in mind during cases. This meant collaborating with all parties involved – clients, families of clients, victims, and the prosecution in criminal cases. "My dad is someone who calls on people to lay down their arms, and he tries to impart as much wisdom as he can to his opponent. To defuse situations, he'll say things like, 'We don't need to do this over and over again. I've done this for 30 years now, and it's just going to end up in the same place,'" he explained.

According to Barry, an important aspect of seeing the big picture is keeping clients' families in mind. He taught Bennett to remember that family members may suffer based on the outcome of verdicts, so that impact is a huge consideration in how cases play out. Bennett commented, "My dad's perspective is almost a protest of our culture, which says that an attorney should be in scorched earth, fight-to-win mode. Most of the time, it's a matter of resolving cases through a discussion with all relevant parties. It takes a village. He's taught me to look at all the factors."

Keeping His Career in Balance

Another crucial lesson absent from Bennett's textbooks has been the importance of not letting his emerging career overwhelm his life. He explained, "The law will take from you whatever it can, whatever you're willing to give it. You can so easily crank away the hours on cases, giving away your emotional and mental strength. And, some lawyers believe that's what's required – even if it means the breakdown of their families, divorce, alcohol abuse, drug abuse. My dad instilled in me that I must take time for myself, my wife, my family, and to understand my limits because the job will always be here. He doesn't stay late at the office or work on weekends. And, he's shown me how to be in the moment, enjoying the little things, like a cup of coffee or leaves changing in the fall."

Bennett added, "The law is full of folks laboring to achieve a result to derive confirmation of their ego, affirmation that they are good enough, smart enough, that they matter. But, that's a never-ending pursuit." Instead, he has learned from Barry that what matters in law at the end of the day is making a human connection.

Sorting Out Their Roles Over Time

Their mentor-mentee, father-son relationship has evolved over time and arrived at a place where Barry and Bennett are now collaborative partners in the firm. But, it was a rocky road getting there. Bennett explained that, when he started the APR 6 program, he struggled between wanting to emulate Barry "in order to be a great lawyer" and finding his own way. He observed, "Parts of me are like my dad, but I have also wanted to try things for myself. When first working with him, if he said not to do something, I would just do it anyway because I've always been like that with him. I wanted to poke the bear. Or, I would say, 'Just let me do it my way, even though I might still end up where you are.' In his wisdom, he understood there were times when it was okay to let me try something that I needed to experience for myself."

Occasionally these conversations turned into arguments. Bennett would tell Barry that he didn't know what he was talking about, and Barry would reply that he had run a successful practice for 25 years before Bennett arrived at the firm. Then, Bennett would say, "That's fine. But, I'm here now. That needs to change. We're not doing that anymore." Barry's response would be, "When you pass the bar exam and become a lawyer, we can do things your way." And, Bennett would think to himself, "Watch this!"

Bennett did complete the APR 6 program in four years, and he passed the bar exam on the first attempt in July 2017. He became licensed the following Christmas season.

As Bennett was advancing toward these milestones, father and son gradually sorted out their roles. Bennett explained, "My dad eventually came to appreciate the importance of me developing my own identity, which was a big part of the APR 6 program – understanding that I could be me and still be a great lawyer. I didn't have to be exactly like my dad. That's a hard realization when your mentor is your father, who you idolize, but who also frustrates you."

While their role clarification developed over time, the perception of Barry and Bennett in the Vancouver legal community also evolved. Initially, other lawyers and judges would greet Bennett by saying, "Oh, you're Barry's son." But, the relationship dynamic is starting to change. More recently, judges might say to Barry, "I was hoping your associate was going to show up."

Bennett commented, "There's certainly a shift happening. I think my dad couldn't be happier that I haven't copied his role, but have learned who I am. He's enjoyed watching me discover myself."

Regarding his self-discovery, Bennett reflected, "I've learned that it doesn't matter what others think. I'm not going to seek affirmation that way, which is a trap in being a lawyer. And, I'm a Type 3 on the Enneagram – the achiever, so my natural bent is to gain affirmation through achievement. I've had to work on that because it's dangerous in this job."

Growing Closer Emotionally

The dance of sorting out their professional roles has led Barry and Bennett to grow much closer emotionally. Bennett explained, "Our relationship has evolved because I have such a deep, humble, thankful heart for my dad. I know that he's a person who is doing a very hard job. And, as a father, he tries to do it all. I've told him that he doesn't have to do it all.

Our relationship has blossomed because I've continued to be more open with him about my emotional side. Consequently, he's opened up to me about his emotional side. I sometimes imagine my ten-year-old self interacting with my dad's ten-year-old self. We are just grown up versions of our childhood selves. We carry those early experiences into our adult lives. We definitely appreciate who the other person is. My dad is not me, and I'm not him."

They've reaped the benefits of their deeper relationship in their work. Bennett commented that Barry's open door policy means that "at the drop of a hat, he covers for me." And, today, Bennett doesn't always ask for his dad's opinion. On the other hand, he commented, "It's very humbling when my dad comes to me and says, 'I need your opinion on this. What do you think?' My role has turned into being a good friend to my dad. Being alone in this job, which he did for many years, was very hard. So, when my dad now asks me for help, I need to have my stuff together to be a resource to him. There's a little co-dependency. We work files together and figure out our case roles that way."

And, they regularly remind each other that their value isn't based on their external achievements. Bennett explained, "Today, I find myself almost mentoring my dad, saying, 'Your worth doesn't come from what people observe you doing on a case. Your worth is in how you relate to these people in jail. That's where you get to be yourself.'" The son has learned well from the father.

Realizing His Calling

Bennett believes his law career is "a divine calling." When he started questioning a psychology career, he "did a significant amount of prayer and meditation" about his future. He recalled, "There was a definite feeling one day of waking up and realizing I was supposed to do this program with my dad." That realization was especially meaningful because Bennett initially wanted another attorney – a family friend – to mentor him through APR 6. But, then he learned the Washington State Bar Association required mentors to also be the employers of mentees. So, Barry became Bennett's employer and mentor.

He described his complicated feelings during the program. "As frustrated as I was at times having my dad mentor me, I needed to be faithful to this because I felt called to do it, even though I didn't know what the calling meant at the time. If we hadn't gone through the program together, we wouldn't have worked through our father-son issues. Who in life gets to do that with your parent?"

The full significance of his calling gradually became clear as Bennett realized he was doing psychology every day in his client work. He cited a current example. "I have to go to the jail tomorrow morning at 8:15 and talk to a client who's probably going to prison about what his options are based on the decisions he's made in the past. It's not so much legal analysis as it is counseling. So, if I hadn't fulfilled my calling, my life would still have been good. But, it wouldn't have been this good."

Trusting in the Future

Bennett and Barry don't have a long-term plan for what happens when the father decides to retire. According to Bennett, Barry wants to "slow down in five years or so." But, Bennett quickly added, "He said that five years ago!"

These days, Barry tells Bennett, "I'll work with you as long as you're willing to tolerate me." And, for his part, Bennett said he feels "terrified because I can't do this alone. I don't know what I'd do without my dad."

Bennett thinks a lot about his future as he's managing cases and continuing to learn from Barry. He explained, "I ask myself what I'm going to do. That answer hasn't come yet. But, I'm trying to be receptive to signs of new opportunities. My career might take a different shape. My job is to be responsive, loyal to my calling, and willing to say I'll follow through with that. That's what got me here. It's hard to remain open-minded, but the beauty is in not knowing what's going to happen tomorrow. I definitely want to show up for it."

Emerging from the Dust of His Rabbi

Bennett used a metaphor to capture the essence of his mentoring experience under Barry. "There's a concept in ancient Jewish tradition of a young student learning scripture to become a rabbi being covered in the dust of the rabbi. The idea was the student followed the rabbi so closely that he'd be covered in the dust from his rabbi's footsteps. You're trying to emulate this person, but you still have to take your own journey and discover yourself. Your mentor won't always be there. At some point, you have to take the work further on your own."

CHAPTER 5

FULFILLING HER CALLING
AS A CHILD EDUCATOR

*"Ursula's passion resonated with something in me that
got me going down my path. I hadn't been particularly
interested in becoming a teacher. She was very
instrumental in my life. I still have dreams about her."*

❧

REBECCA KEITH WAS in her early 20s when she
and her husband, an artist and maker of musical
instruments, were raising two very young children. It was 1972, and the family lived in Redwood City,
California. She recalled the challenging time. "We were really
strapped financially, so while I thought it was important to
stay at home with the kids, I realized that I was going to have
to find some way to help support our family."

Little did she know that her two-year-old son, Seth,
would lead her to the solution. Rebecca's mother was a teacher,
and her father was a child psychoanalyst and professor. So,

she was attuned to children's developmental needs and the importance of giving them a stimulating learning environment. She described Seth's toddler behavior. "At this young age, it was obvious that he was destined for math or engineering. He took everything apart, anything that moved. Then one day he was sitting in my lap, and we were talking about the pictures in a book he was holding. Suddenly he said, 'No, no, no, no, no,' pointed to the page number, and asked, 'What's that?' I said to myself, 'Oh, dear! My child needs something that I don't have!'"

This motivated Rebecca to seek educational resources for Seth beyond what she and any nursery school could provide. She recounted, "That's when I found Montessori. Seth went to half day preschool for a year between ages two and three at the Montessori International School down the hill from where we lived. I became enamored with the environment, materials, and what the school offered. I have never been happy with traditional education. I thought kids wasted a lot of time in school. I used to have books hidden inside of books because I had already read the assigned books, so why were we reading them again in class? When I discovered Montessori, I thought this is what education should be."

The alternative child education method, which is practiced around the world, had been developed by the pioneering pediatrician and psychiatrist turned educator, Maria Montessori. After working with developmentally disabled, mentally ill, and physically disabled children, she launched her first school for children who were healthy but poor, the Casa dei Bambini, in Rome in 1907. Maria's teaching methods, which have evolved over time, focus on developing a child's initiative and innate abilities, largely through practical play at the child's own pace.[11]

Meeting the Needs of Child and Mother

Rebecca realized that Montessori was just the ticket for two-year-old Seth because it would enhance his natural curiosity about how objects worked and the world of numbers. And, it turned out to be the right decision. Today Seth is a successful computer engineer.

But, enrolling her son in Montessori dramatically shaped Rebecca's life too. It opened a door that led to her lifelong career as a Montessori educator. She described how this unfolded. "While Seth attended preschool, they started running a summer program and needed help with the kids at the pool. I was a lifeguard at the time, and I offered to help with the program as long as I could bring along my younger daughter, Johanna. The staff told me that I was a natural with kids and that I really needed to do this. They said they'd give me a job as a classroom assistant if I took the training. I was enamored with Montessori, and it made total sense to pursue as a career because it would fit with my kids' schedules." So, Rebecca became a classroom assistant in the fall of 1973.

She continued, "Of course, working as an assistant, I didn't even make enough money to pay for Seth and Johanna to go there. But, I found Montessori so engaging that I started investigating where I could take my teacher training. That's how I met Ursula Thrush, who would become my mentor."

---

11 "Maria Montessori," Wikipedia. Accessed November 18, 2019. https://en.wikipedia.org/wiki/Maria_Montessori.

Rejecting the Safe Choice to Follow Her Heart

By 1973, two Montessori training centers in the San Francisco Bay Area were affiliated with international organizations for certification – a center in Palo Alto affiliated with the Association Montessori Internationale (AMI) and a center in San Leandro affiliated with the American Montessori Society (AMS). In addition, Ursula had founded the Maria Montessori School of the Golden Gate and Teacher Training Center in San Francisco in 1972.

Rebecca explained why she chose Ursula's training center. "I checked out all three options. Ursula was in the process of becoming affiliated with AMI, but that hadn't happened yet. So, it was risky taking training with her. However, after interviewing her, I felt she was so much more in tune with what mattered to me. Her enthusiasm, energy, dedication, love of what she did, and deep understanding of the Montessori philosophy really spoke to me. There was an electricity, a magnetism about her. It made me want to train with her instead of the more established centers, even though it was a longer drive to San Francisco than Palo Alto."

"I have no idea how I managed to juggle everything. I had a three-and-a-half-year-old and a two-year-old who were attending the Montessori school in Redwood City, where I was assisting. And, I was taking my training up in San Francisco over two years with six hours of course work and six hours of lab work every week," Rebecca recalled.

Pursuing Their Passion: Mentor and Mentee

She shared the background of her mentor – the woman who deeply influenced Rebecca's own Montessori journey. Born in Budapest, Hungary, in 1930, Ursula grew up as an only child and watched her country change hands during World War II. As a "drop dead gorgeous" young woman, she married a diplomat, and they had one son, Ray. When the family was stationed in London, Ursula experienced an identity crisis, feeling that her life lacked something.

According to Rebecca, "Her husband didn't understand what was happening to her. One day, Ursula walked past a Montessori school and was drawn to go inside. She became totally immersed and took her primary training in London, then went on to Bergamo, Italy, for her elementary training. There she trained with Maria Montessori's son, Mario. So, Ursula's roots went back almost to the source. She also had a Ph.D. in philosophy."

Ursula deeply believed in the Montessori mission of "education for peace and changing the world through education." Rebecca explained that Ursula saw the connection between Montessori and peace as "making the child the best she or he can be, therefore making the world a better place because it's inhabited by fully developed people."

That passion drove Ursula to dramatically transform her life. "She had inherited from her grandparents a huge secretary's desk that was very ornate with lots of cubbyholes and secret compartments. She loved it, and it was the only thing she personally owned. Ursula sold the desk to get the money to take her training. That's how much she felt this was an important thing to do," Rebecca recounted.

In 1968, Ursula left her husband and came to San Francisco with her son to start a new life as a Montessori educator. She taught at Gateway Montessori before starting her own school in 1972. Her mentor, Mario, encouraged her to open a training center that same year as well. She later became involved with the founders of the Montessori Accreditation Council for Teacher Education (MACTE), which oversaw school accreditation. Rebecca elaborated, "She was very engaged in making sure education for peace was included in the approved curriculum and traveled around to training centers to monitor that. Ursula also attended Montessori conferences around the world. She was dominant in her field."

Rebecca described her mentor's magnetism. "She was quite a character, which was part of her appeal. Very opinionated and strong-willed, she had a mighty temper. You had to be careful not to piss her off. But, she was also energetic and dedicated. She used to say to me, 'Montessori is so important to the world. If this is your calling, you will feel it as strongly as I did, and you can really make a difference.'"

Rebecca did feel it was her calling, and she wholeheartedly committed to Montessori in her early 20s. She reminisced, "We used to say we were closet revolutionaries because we saw Montessori as a non-violent way to solve problems at the time of the Vietnam War."

Learning the Montessori Method

Ursula personally trained Rebecca, who described the Montessori classroom as "a prepared environment, which is very important with each activity having a direct and an indirect aim. The activities are arranged in sequence to prepare the child for the next activity." Montessori classroom environments are organized in five sections – practical life, sensorial experience, culture, math, and language.

"She showed me how to use every piece of apparatus in the classroom and how to transmit concepts embodied in concrete materials to the child in a way that the child comes to understand the concepts independently," Rebecca explained.

One example is the materials used for a sensorial exercise that embodies the concept of large vs. small. The child plays with a block of rectangular, polished wood that holds 10 cylinders, each with a knob on the top. And, the cylinders fit into the block in a graduated order from smaller to larger diameters and heights. First the child removes the cylinders from the block by the knobs. At that point, the cylinders are in random order. "The only way the child can put the cylinders back into the holes and put the block back on the shelf is to figure out which is the smallest cylinder, then the next smallest, until placing all the cylinders in order. You want to show the child how to use the piece of apparatus without taking away the excitement of discovery. The goal is to help rather than perform the task for the child," Rebecca explained.

This was a fundamental teaching technique that she learned from Ursula. She elaborated, "There's a way to seduce a child to use a piece of apparatus and know when to step away and not interrupt the child's concentration. Ursula helped me develop the skills to observe children."

Absorbing Lessons in Multiple Ways

Rebecca's learning was through direct explanations from Ursula and by watching her mentor. This included a wide range of skills and activities, such as conducting parent-teacher conferences and parent education meetings. Rebecca also absorbed lessons from Ursula's many accomplishments. She recalled, "Sometimes I learned from observing her that I wouldn't do it the same way as Ursula. Nevertheless, she was a great role model, being a single woman on her own with a child in a country where she wasn't born. She was amazingly articulate in English, running her own business and training center, and a passionate speaker. She was charismatic. People were drawn to her."

New challenges also created learning opportunities. "Ursula would constantly throw me into slightly bigger ponds all the time, like doing a presentation at a Montessori conference. She would say, 'Get your act together and go do it.' She would challenge me to move from my comfort zone to something a little bit scarier," Rebecca reminisced.

She continued, "It's important to find the right balance between challenge and support when mentoring others. And, the right balance varies from person to person. I learned this by observing how Ursula interacted with me and others. This helped me be a better mentor over the years."

The balance between mentor challenge and support is a Montessori theme that transfers over to interacting with the children. "The goal is to be there to support the child while she or he is becoming more and more independent – intellectually and emotionally. And, it's a symbiotic relationship.

As Montessori teachers, we receive as much as we give," Rebecca explained.

At the core of Rebecca's training was learning how to show up for the children. She explained that Montessori teachers need to be "physically, emotionally, and spiritually present. This means having practices to follow so we can leave our stuff outside the door and walk into the classroom fully present." Such practices differ for everyone, Rebecca explained. "It might be taking a walk, listening to music, yoga, meditation. For example, Ursula did guided meditations with us as one option," she added.

Coming into Her Own

Rebecca trained with Ursula from 1973 to 1975. She also worked in Ursula's school from fall 1974 to spring/summer 1976. Then, Rebecca faced a challenge in her relationship with Ursula that forced a crucial career decision.

She shared the story. "Ursula always emphasized the importance of dedication and passion – being true to what you believed in and willing to take risks. In the fall of 1976, she wanted me to start a new, experimental kindergarten classroom at her school. But, at that point, I only had two years of classroom experience, and the Montessori philosophy was to stay in the same classroom environment with the same children for three years. I strongly believed that was important in order to fine-tune my techniques. So, I told Ursula I couldn't start the new kindergarten classroom. She responded, 'Then, I guess you're not going to work for me!'"

So, Rebecca left Ursula's nest and found a teaching job at the Country Lane Montessori School in Monte Sereno,

California, where she taught from 1976 to 1979. She recalled that "it was very risky to do that because we were always teetering financially." But, Rebecca took the leap because she fervently believed in the importance of developing her skills in an established classroom before setting up her own classroom. "I had to be willing to do what Montessori taught and not compromise for expediency," she commented.

In the end, the relationship survived and thrived. Rebecca explained, "Ursula was pissed at me. But, after getting angry, she could let it go, and I was able to handle it. We reconnected less as student-teacher and more like peers – certainly colleagues." And, their relationship deepened over many more years.

She reflected on what the relationship shift meant in the long run. "To come into my own, I had to go away because Ursula was such a strong personality. There was no way I was going to able to make my own mistakes and continue at her school. Although Ursula was upset that I left, she was able to listen and respect my decision. As a mentor, you have to be able to let your mentee follow her own path."

Achieving Career Milestones

After everything she had learned from Ursula and benefitting from their ongoing relationship, in 1979 Rebecca was ready to truly strike out on her own. She opened the One World Montessori School in San Jose, California, with a single classroom of 40 children. Having achieved that milestone, she also started helping Ursula in her Maria Montessori Teacher Training Center (MMTTC) in San Francisco.

In 1986, Rebecca and a partner launched the nonprofit

organization, Montessori Phoenix Project. The mission was to train teachers in impoverished areas of Mexico and Nicaragua to start their own schools. Sponsors provided the program funding. And, the work continued for approximately 16 years.

Over the years, Rebecca also gradually took on increasingly greater responsibility at the MMTTC. And, she began preparing to lead the MMTTC, which involved a long journey to complete her own formal education. Rebecca earned a Bachelor of Arts in human and community services in 2006, a Master of Arts in educational leadership in 2008, and a doctorate in educational leadership in 2014 – all from Saint Mary's College in Moraga, California.

In 2002, while working toward her bachelor's degree, she assumed leadership of the training center. Rebecca moved the MMTTC to San Jose near her school in 2004. At that point, One World Montessori had grown to around 250 students at three campuses. Rebecca also assisted in opening a branch of the MMTTC in Santa Rosa, California.

Today One World Montessori has three campuses in San Jose serving 200 children. And, Rebecca now leads her school remotely from Camas, Washington, where she moved in 2015. She travels to San Jose a few times a month, and she trains by hosting teacher workshops in her home and using internet meeting technology for remote sessions. These days, she focuses on the Montessori philosophy, psychology, and classroom management and leaves materials training to others. However, as of this writing, the future of her school is uncertain due to changes required by the state of California to mitigate the risks of COVID-19.

Cherishing Amazing Experiences

Rebecca shared stories about her richest memories of Ursula. In the early 1990s, her mentor was part of a group of 25 colleagues, including Rebecca, who took a two-week, international trip that traced Maria Montessori's journey from Italy to India to Amsterdam. "We started in Rome and visited the Casa dei Bambini, where Maria started her first school. It was thrilling to see those hallowed halls! The school was still operating. A favorite memory was a dinner in a cavernous, dimly lit Roman restaurant. We were seated around a long table. The 'Macarena' was all the rage, and that music started playing. Being the life of the party, Ursula bounded up on the table and got the rest of us up there dancing with her!"

Next the group toured India, where Maria and her son, Mario, had lived for a number of years giving training courses and lecturing. When Italy entered World War II as a German ally, Italians in India were interned by Britain since the country was a British colony. Mario was interned for two months before being allowed to join Maria, who had to reside on the Theosophical Society compound, where she had been delivering training courses. However, they had permission to travel for lectures and training.[12]

India was especially significant for Ursula, Rebecca, and the others because Maria's work had been influenced by the Indian philosopher, Sri Aurobindo. "We visited his ashram to learn more about the connections that Maria had made there," Rebecca recalled. Aurobindo's philosophy focused on the stages of evolving consciousness. And, Maria's philosophy

12 "Maria Montessori," Wikipedia. Accessed November 18, 2019. https://en.wikipedia.org/wiki/Maria_Montessori.

addressed growth of the child to increasingly higher levels through self-discipline.

Their last stop was Amsterdam, where Maria lived after the war. She is buried in the nearby seaside town, Noordwijk. The group visited her grave and stood in awe to reflect on her many achievements. Maria's tombstone reads, "I beg the dear, all powerful children to join me in creating peace in man and in the world." Rebecca reminisced, "We all vowed at that moment to do our part to assist in this mighty endeavor."

Aside from their travels, Rebecca fondly remembered socializing with Ursula over the years. "After her son had grown and moved to Thailand, she spent time with our family. She came to our home for Thanksgiving and to our kids' weddings. I had known her almost my entire adult life."

She continued, "A favorite thing we would do is sit around after dinner with a glass of wine and discuss Montessori philosophy. We would talk about the phases of development, what were the most important things we could do to fulfill a child's potential, and how to transfer those ideas to the adults we were training to be teachers. A big question was how to meet the developmental needs of adult students. During these late-night conversations, we were trying to better understand the nature of learning and human beings."

Being Together at the End

After a long relationship, Ursula and Rebecca were together at the end. "Ursula got cancer. I would visit her in her home, where she insisted on staying rather than receiving treatment, and I would bring pictures of my grandchildren. I tried to help her through her transition toward death. And, in the end, I sat outside her hospital room waiting for the doctor to make sure she got the care that she needed."

Rebecca continued, "The night before she died, I was at the hospital until 11 p.m. Then, I went home and fell asleep. I awakened at 4 a.m., woke up my husband, and said to him, 'Ursula just died.' Then, I called the hospital and got confirmation."

She processed her grief by getting busy arranging Ursula's memorial service in the church adjacent to her mentor's San Francisco school. Rebecca organized the music, food, speakers, and guest list. She also "got a bunch of people together to sing peace songs, which was an appropriate remembrance of Ursula."

The keynote speaker for the service, Dr. Feland Meadows, was a man with whom Rebecca later collaborated on Montessori activities. "So, Ursula continued providing connections for me even after she was gone," Rebecca observed.

Reflecting on Ursula's Influence

She acknowledged the role that Ursula had played in the international Montessori community. "Her contribution was in the area of education for peace. She lit a spark in so many people. She truly felt that if our developmental needs could be fully met at all stages, we'd be a much more peaceful species. That concept hadn't been well articulated, and Ursula made it more concrete. She also ensured it was embedded in the Montessori curriculum and teacher training centers. Ursula was a gift to so many people."

And, Rebecca reflected on her mentor's role in her own life. "Ursula's passion resonated with something in me that got me going down my path. I hadn't been particularly interested in becoming a teacher. She was very instrumental in my life. I still have dreams about her."

CHAPTER 6

NAVIGATING A UNIVERSITY SYSTEM

*"I feel extremely fortunate with Jean-Pierre to
have learned how to live in this world."*

⊷

J OHN GREENE WAS a brand new Docteur de
l'Universite from the University of Grenoble, France,
in June 1968. Then, he crossed the Pond and joined
the French Department at the University of Victoria, British
Columbia, in September of that year. A native of Edmonton,
Alberta, John recalled that Victoria "was my first choice
because I had family there, so I knew the area."

He started out teaching first and second year French to
intermediate students who already had "some grounding in
French." Unlike prior teaching with his master's degree, he
described his initial Victoria classroom experience as "quite a
shock because maybe six out of 30 students actually wanted
to study French." John was not prepared for the student
hostility that he faced. Freshmen and sophomores were sub-
jected to two years of French upon entering the university

because of a universal language requirement. Many of them felt stuck in French classes when they desperately wanted to learn other subjects.

He had gotten caught up in a political battle. Some faculty members, including John, were advocating moving the universal language requirement back to the high schools as a university prerequisite. Others fought to preserve the requirement at the university because it provided teaching assistant jobs. After three years, the controversy was finally resolved by setting a new admission requirement of some language knowledge in all but a few programs of study.

Bonding with a Kindred Spirit

In these rocky, early days, John met the man who was to be his mentor over the next 25 years. Jean-Pierre Mentha, a senior faculty member in the French Department, was "open, friendly, helpful, and not the university type." The relationship developed organically as there was no formal mentoring program. Naturally gregarious and always ready with a joke, Jean-Pierre was an accomplished language professor throughout Canada in the 1940s and 1950s. His magnetism attracted multiple faculty and student mentees over many years.

John recalled finding a kindred spirit in Jean-Pierre. "I very much enjoyed chatting with him in the corridors, and we clicked right away. We would often have engaging discussions in between meetings." They agreed early on that teaching students was the primary purpose of the university and that research was secondary. John described this perspective as "anathema to a lot of faculty, who viewed students as a necessary evil" in contrast to publishing research.

Among John's favorite memories of Jean-Pierre were the regular occasions when his mentor invited colleagues and students into his home for lively discussions on a wide range of subjects over coffee or drinks. "We chatted about everything. It was such a friendly atmosphere to converse with someone who shared so much wisdom."

Witnessing a Consummate Educator

Jean-Pierre's career trajectory was "on a bit of a sidetrack," John recalled. His mentor was Swiss and spoke four or five languages since his childhood. As a native speaker, Jean-Pierre's language skills were highly sought in universities. At Victoria, he taught advanced French to senior students, including oral and expository writing skills. But, this specialization proved to be a career obstacle in the Victoria system. John commented, "Later in Jean-Pierre's career, we had quite a fight to get him promoted. But, he was well established, and everybody respected him. So, he was eventually promoted to Associate Professor."

Despite his promotion challenges, Jean-Pierre was a consummate educator. He passed along many important tips to John on how to teach practical things. John cited an example. "The French word 'y' is an indirect object pronoun that applies only to things, not people, and is confusing to English speakers. Jean-Pierre gave students specific rules on when to use this pronoun that were way better than any textbook." This and numerous other tips from Jean-Pierre inspired John to create some of his own rules that eased the learning process. After John later became the department chair, he used many of his mentor's teaching techniques to help younger faculty. "Of course, Jean-Pierre was always there to consult about rules," John added.

Learning Emotional Intelligence

Jean-Pierre's language skills combined with his emotional intelligence served him well as a mentor to John and others. John remembers him as fun-loving and calm with a talent for light conversation that put people at ease. "He was sympathetic to the problems of students and faculty. At the same time, he was very clear minded and would not tolerate nonsense. He would cut if off because he didn't suffer fools. Yet, he never held anything against you and was able to keep professional disagreements separate from his personal interactions. That was in contrast to other faculty members who were very invested in their ideas."

Of all his strengths, Jean-Pierre's empathy stands out in John's memory. "He was so good at understanding a person's feelings, which allowed him to help them deal with issues, especially how the institution worked and how to make your way through the system. He didn't let his emotions get in the way of clearly seeing situations," John recalled.

John shared a favorite story to illustrate this. He and the department chairman had both been on sabbatical, so another administrator temporarily led the department, which had received an important grant. This temporary administrator decided on his own to redirect the department's grant money to purchase audiovisual equipment for the entire university. When John discovered this upon his return, he was outraged that funds he had anticipated for his language center had been misappropriated. "I figured that we had been ripped off, and I was hot under the collar. I started gathering all the documents I could find, intending to report the incident to the department chair and the media."

But, Jean-Pierre saved John from himself. "He helped me see that I could have done a lot of damage to myself because whistleblowers usually get punished. He taught me to work through the chain of command by going to the dean, who talked to the vice president. After I did that, the dean came up with other funding to help me get the things that I wanted. I later became assistant to the dean, so I was better able to push the language department agenda. By following Jean-Pierre's advice, I used the system properly and got more back than I would have by making a minor public scandal." John had learned the important lesson of letting his emotions cool down to make rational decisions and navigate the system.

Jean-Pierre's emotional lessons started early in their relationship. Having graduated at the top of his class ever since high school, John described himself as "arrogant" when he first joined Victoria. "I came in with a big chip on my shoulder, but Jean-Pierre quickly let me know that other people around me had figured out some things too. He pointed out my limitations and taught me to use my actual abilities to my advantage. I learned humility. He was gently firm."

But, toning down arrogance didn't mean that John became a pushover. He also learned from Jean-Pierre the importance of standing up to bullies without yelling. John described his predecessor department chair as "irascible and universally disliked." The chair would routinely try to bait John with blaming statements, false assertions, and weak claims. But, John skillfully defused the negativity by consistently and deliberately addressing the chair's behavior. He learned to keep the chair under control by asserting himself with civility. The best tribute to this lesson from Jean-Pierre came when the former chair toasted John at his retirement with the words, "He was a velvet hand in a velvet glove."

Jean-Pierre became an important happiness role model to John. "He was happy because his wife and kids were the center of his life, and he also thoroughly enjoyed his students and colleagues. I learned from him that my early ambitions were not necessary and that I could make the life I wanted in the system if I learned to navigate it. He knocked a bit of youthful arrogance out of me and showed me how to be helpful to people and get what I wanted."

Paying it Forward

In the late 1970s, inspired by Jean-Pierre's mentorship, John "pushed the department to hire senior students to spend an hour a week with small groups of incoming students. I knew that much more than French lessons would happen. We funded the program with government grants. By the time I was department chair, we brought in more than my salary in grants every year. This program was still active when I retired."

Growing the Relationship

Over time, John became increasingly more comfortable contributing to his conversations with Jean-Pierre. And, the dynamic of their relationship began shifting when John advanced to department chair. He also took on administrative roles at the university level, which gave him influence in the offices of the dean and vice president. Jean-Pierre respected John's influence and would sometimes ask him to "drop a word" with the right administrator to advocate for a departmental interest. They had become equals in collaborating to leverage John's institutional influence for the department's benefit.

Long-term friendship was the natural outgrowth of the time they spent together. Sharing many common interests and passions, John and Jean-Pierre started extending invitations to each other's homes within the first five years of their relationship. John reminisced, "We got together with anywhere from four to eight people, usually at Jean-Pierre's home, five or six times a year. This continued well beyond his retirement. While we did a certain amount of plotting about internal university politics, our gatherings were mostly about our lives and plans, what we were reading, and of course a bit of personal gossip and national politics."

Internalizing Life Lessons

John has no doubt that having Jean-Pierre in his life made it much better. "Without him, I would have had a harder time dealing with things at the university and would have made more mistakes. I would have been much more focused on myself and my desire for promotions. I would have been less happy and free. He had a huge, positive impact on me." John cited the big lessons as humility, kindness, empathy for everyone, justice, intellectual rigor, and staying involved.

In reviewing a draft of this chapter, John shared, "I was struck by how much Jean-Pierre resembled my father in temperament. As I desired Jean-Pierre's approval, but did not need it on an existential level, and as he delivered suggestions rather than correctives, I was able to internalize with him lessons that I had already received from my father, but had previously resisted."

While John also enjoyed his relationships with other departmental colleagues, and they frequently "talked things out," these relationships "didn't carry the same weight." Jean-Pierre played a uniquely important role.

Moving on After Jean-Pierre

After Jean-Pierre retired in the early 1990s, John started winding down his own career. He stopped taking roles outside the department. After returning from a one-year compassionate leave of absence to care for his sick wife, John shared the chair role with the dean on an interim, one-year basis. From there John continued part-time until he retired in 2009.

Summing up his career at Victoria and the influence of his mentor, John said, "I feel extremely fortunate with Jean-Pierre to have learned how to live in this world. It's such a shame there isn't a lot more helpfulness coming to young people all the time. It's a hard world to navigate, especially if you don't have excellent examples. I feel privileged to have had this."

CHAPTER 7

GROWING INTO HER WHOLE SELF

*"If I hadn't met Jeannie, I wouldn't have been introduced
to Jungian psychology. I would not have had the feminine
holding presence that she gave me, and I really needed that…
She was another mother experience – mother as mentor."*

❧

THERESE BROOKS WAS advancing toward a major life threshold, but she didn't know it. She finished her second degree in anthropology at age 29 – after completing a prior English degree. By her early 30s, she was married with two young daughters, living in Florida, and holding down part-time jobs as a pharmaceutical salesperson and a server.

She recalled the emptiness in her heart. "I felt sad and was making a big adjustment to having two young girls. My beloved grandmother was dying. I was still getting used to being married and didn't really like it. Having a lot of curiosity and loving school, I was looking for somewhere to be amused again intellectually. I wanted to take classes without pursuing another degree. I was a wife, mother, daughter, and granddaughter, but I was kind of lost."

Then in 1996 at age 36, she found the Jung Center in Winter Park, Florida. The center offered a range of classes in Jungian psychology, also known as depth psychology. The field had been developed by the pioneering psychiatrist and visionary, Dr. Carl Jung. Therese signed up for Jeannie Raffa's class on dreams. "I wasn't interested in dreams per se, but the class was available on the only day that I could arrange for childcare. However, I was blown away, awestruck by her class." Thanks to serendipity, due to her childcare schedule, Therese had met the woman who would introduce dreams as the gateway to the unconscious and would evolve into her first and formative mentor.

Her introduction to Jung via the dream class opened a whole world that Therese hadn't known existed. "After completing the dream class, I took another class with Jeannie on the Goddess. Then I took every class the center offered with every teacher. I also worked privately with Jeannie on analyzing my dreams. She was not a therapist. But, as a teacher, author, and lecturer, she had a profound grasp of Jungian psychology. Jeannie had written books on her own dreaming experiences and how she came to know herself through her unconscious," Therese explained.

Embracing the Goddess

She continued, "At some point in Jeannie's life, she put down assumptions about who she was supposed to be and started becoming who she was meant to be. Raised in a traditional religious background, she always had a connection to that.

But, it was obvious that the feminine was missing. So, she really embraced this notion of the Goddess." Therese defined the Goddess as a Jungian archetype (a basic, universal symbol or image) that represents "the feminine, queenly, relational, mothering, nurturing aspect and balances the masculine concept of god as hierarchical and authoritarian – the king."

On an ever-evolving journey to explore the inner life of her soul, Jeannie had become a respected Jungian scholar. Her first two books included *Dream Theatres of the Soul: Empowering the Feminine through Jungian Dream Work* and *The Bridge to Wholeness: A Feminine Alternative to the Hero Myth*. She later published *Healing the Sacred Divide: Making Peace with Ourselves, Each Other, and the World*. A doctorate in curriculum and instruction from the University of Florida had been the foundation of Jeannie's teaching, lecturing, and writing.

As their relationship evolved over 10+ years, Therese increasingly took in Jeannie's knowledge and wisdom within the Goddess framework. This unfolded during classes, their private dream work, and other activities. Therese also worked as Jeannie's assistant, handling administrative tasks like class registration. And, she provided feedback on Jeannie's manuscript for *Healing the Sacred Divide*.

Experiencing Jeannie

Therese described Jeannie and the rich experience of learning from her. "This tall, thin, beautiful woman with hair turning silver was married to a man who adored her and fully supported her writing ability."

Jeannie, in turn, nurtured Therese's creative side.

"Although my English degree was about poetry and literature, which was artistic and deeply satisfying, there was this tension in academia to emphasize and give greater validity to the scientific, which is very masculine. In my anthropology studies, I unconsciously adopted that scientific mindset. So, when I met Jeannie, it seemed like I could recover and let go of some masculine striving," Therese reflected.

Learning from Jeannie was experiential, not theoretical. "Making masks in her classes was delightful. And, some classes took place in her beautiful, old Victorian home. She had a collection of blue glass on her mantle and a lot of art everywhere. There was a sensuousness to her home and to her."

"At one point early in our relationship, Jeannie said that she valued our relationship and enjoyed mentoring me. I hadn't created that sort of identity for myself. I thought of our work together as a hobby. But, we were analyzing my dreams, and so much of my unconscious was coming up that she knew how to work with. She was a natural."

Unconsciously Growing

While Therese hadn't yet identified her future career as a Jungian-oriented psychotherapist, her work with Jeannie was laying the essential foundation. Her mentor led Therese on a personal development journey of exploring her soul through dreams and archetypes – especially the Goddess. In Jungian terms, Therese was on a path to individuating – becoming her whole self, integrating her feminine and masculine aspects. She recalled, "Without Jeannie, I don't think I could have developed myself to do my work as a psychotherapist. It was crucial experience and education. Yet, what was happening with Jeannie was still very unconscious at the time."

Therese explained that her dream work with Jeannie focused on looking at her shadow – a Jungian term for the unconscious, unknown aspects of the personality.

"I started to become aware of family of origin issues, such as early childhood trauma, the messages that had been transmitted to me from my family of origin, and resulting neuroses. I knew that family of origin issues had bothered me. And, I was becoming aware through this dream work – co-dependency, alcoholism, unresolved grief, loss, divorce, feelings of abandonment. These issues had been residing in my unconscious," Therese observed.

Gaining Insights and Skills

Life lessons were an important outcome of their work together. Therese described Jeannie as "kind and loving." She absorbed precious insights about love and grief from her mentor. "Jeannie had become a grandmother and wrote a lot about what that meant to her. And, she had a horse that she deeply loved. She watched her horse suffer and die, so I got to observe Jeannie's way of grieving over deep loss. I had tragic, unresolved loss that hadn't been conscious," Therese reflected. Jeannie's way of being in touch with her feelings left a lasting imprint on Therese and helped her come to terms with her own loss.

Dealing with strong, negative emotions of others was another lesson that would prove invaluable to Therese in her eventual psychotherapy profession. She recalled a time when she and another woman had been discussing their dreams with Jeannie. "The other woman suddenly erupted. She became accusatory and unreasonable. Not everyone is equipped to handle dream work. At first, Jeannie, who always had a lot of poise and grace, was patient with her. But, at some point, she reached her limit of patience and asked the woman to leave the session. I had always been scared of people who behaved with strong, negative emotion and hadn't known how to confront them and remain solid when they were falling apart." Therese learned important lessons from Jeannie about equanimity and setting limits.

In nurturing Therese's growth, Jeannie challenged her to acquire new skills by taking more active roles at the Jung Center. She encouraged Therese to run her own dream groups and to create and teach her own class. "The class that I created was on the mother-daughter initiation into the conscious feminine. My oldest daughter was age nine, and I understood the necessity of giving daughters an experience of something positive about the feminine. So, in my class, we talked about the six Greek Goddess archetypes. We also discussed important passages, such as girls reaching puberty. I thought that would be a good thing to do for daughters," Therese explained.

Deepening the Connection

Therese gradually became acquainted with Jeannie more personally as she witnessed her mentor going through major life transitions. Jeannie would frequently talk about her adult children – a daughter who was earning her Ph.D. in marriage and family therapy and a son who was getting married. And, she shared in Jeannie's joy over becoming a grandparent. "I got to know her husband and kids, and although we weren't family, we were affiliated in a familial way," Therese commented.

She also savored attending workshops at Jeannie's Florida beach home. Therese remembered those occasions as "very cool," explaining that "there was an energy, an essence about Jeannie. She was very safe and authentic to be around."

Continuing to Individuate

Over time, Therese's life took some major turns. She and her family wanted to live on the west coast, so in 2008 they chose the Vancouver, Washington, area for the beautiful landscape and quality of life. Her formative 10+ years with Jeannie in Florida had deeply transformed Therese. She wasn't the same person leaving Florida that she was the day she walked into the Jung Center for the first time. Thanks to Jeannie, Therese's inner life had become essential to her. So, once settled into her Pacific Northwest home, she sought a new dream group. This was a major transition. As Therese's relationship with Jeannie started receding into the background due to life circumstances, she was entering a new phase when her second mentor would appear.

She recounted, "I found a dream group in Tualatin, Oregon. It was run by Martha Blake, a Jungian analyst. I also joined her 26-week *Changing Women* group, and I started analysis with her, which lasted six years. Later I joined some of her other groups, like one on a personality indicator. I liked the group experience. It was very satisfying."

Despite her immersion in Jungian work, Therese still thought of these activities as a hobby. She recalled how that started to change. "One day in an analytic session, Martha said I could do Jungian analysis as a profession because I'd be very good at it. She also noted that Jeannie had been an excellent teacher. I was in my early 50s, and I hadn't thought of getting another degree."

As her analyst, Martha had started mentoring Therese by guiding her to consider how she might continue individuating after her grown children left home. So, Therese began investigating graduate programs and ultimately enrolled in the Pacifica Graduate Institute, which offers residential learning Jungian psychology programs in Carpinteria, California. (Jeannie had written a glowing reference letter for her application.) Therese explained Martha's role in choosing the school. "She helped me realize that I needed to be at Pacifica rather than a different clinical program because Jungian analysis deals with individuation, and she was encouraging my self-development."

Juggling during Transitions

Therese continued in analysis with Martha while attending Pacifica, which required traveling to the campus once a month for two and a half years. She also embarked on a divorce when she had a year left of graduate school. She recalled, "It was a very challenging time. While going through a divorce, I still had to write my thesis and then work two years at a low rate to get enough internship hours to become licensed."

She graduated in 2015 with a Master of Arts in counseling psychology with an emphasis on depth psychology. Then, Martha guided her through the process of completing her internships. But, Martha's role in Therese's professional development didn't end there. "After I graduated, she really encouraged me to continue my studies and become a Jungian analyst (a level of training and certification beyond practicing as a Jungian-oriented psychotherapist). That would be another eight years," Therese explained.

Therese continued juggling major life transitions. She enrolled in the Inter-Regional Society of Jungian Analyst Training in Santa Fe and completed the first-year seminar program. Meanwhile, she was still accumulating hours to complete her internship, finalizing her divorce, and helping one daughter enter graduate school and another daughter start her own business. Then, after becoming licensed and launching her Jungian psychotherapy practice, Therese's work with Martha transitioned from psychoanalysis to training analysis. This meant that she received supervision on her client cases from Martha. She also participated in Martha's consultation group.

But, becoming a full-fledged Jungian analyst was not in the cards. Therese did apply for the next stage of analyst training after completing the first-year seminar. During a day of interviews, it became clear that she would not be accepted into the program. Therese explained, "The interviewers, mostly women, kept asking me why I wanted to become an analyst because I already had so much experience. They thought that I was striving to achieve a certain persona, although they encouraged me to go through a second year of the seminar and then reapply."

She elaborated, "I wanted to be part of a tribe and continue being mentored. In Santa Fe I had interacted with some of the best analysts in the country. These were people who had written books that I really admired. Every instructor had a high level of expertise. But, ultimately, I decided not to pursue analyst training because it was expensive at $1,000 a month in travel expenses and tuition, and it would take years. It would have been exhausting doing that and working full-time."

Imparting Her Own Wisdom

So instead, Therese has continued building her psychotherapy practice in Vancouver. Her clients are mostly women undergoing life transitions. She described her specialty. "I work with women on identity formation. I am a strong feminist, and I bring in the Jungian relational aspects of the feminine. I think of myself as the face of the crone. The three faces of the Goddess, according to Jung, are the maiden, the mother, and the crone."

Identifying with the crone archetype, Therese views her role as imparting wisdom to guide women through the changes that life brings. She has become a mentor to many of her clients. Therese observed, "I've noticed in the women I mentor that if they've had a good mother or grandmother experience, it has really helped a lot." Her own life transitions; her roles as wife, mother, grandmother, and single woman again; and especially her immersion in the Jungian model have shaped her work.

Honoring Their Legacy

Therese gave enormous credit to Jeannie and Martha for their profound influence on her life.

"If I hadn't met Jeannie, I wouldn't have been introduced to Jungian psychology. I would not have had the feminine holding presence that she gave me, and I really needed that because it had not been present for me. My mother has a strong masculine aspect, which is very different from Jeannie. She was another mother experience – mother as mentor. Through Jeannie, I developed a relationship with the Goddess – the feminine aspect of divinity."

And, Therese fully acknowledged Martha for guiding her along her transition path from Jungian psychology as hobby to Jungian psychology as profession. Her individual psychoanalysis and group work with Martha provided the framework from which she ultimately launched her profession. "Martha gave me a lot of really valuable mentoring," she commented.

Jeannie had been her muse, and Martha had been her career guide. So, Therese has stayed in touch with them. While maintaining her relationship with Martha, Therese has also communicated with Jeannie over the years through email and by following her writing in "Matrignosis: A Blog About Inner Wisdom."

Therese reflected on how her life has evolved under her mentors' guidance. "In my earlier life, I did a lot of extroverted thinking. Now, I'm much more about introverted feeling as I'm individuating. That's also life cycle. We spend the first half of our lives making our place in the world. In the second half, we relax into that place and get ready to fold back in."

CHAPTER 8

LEARNING LEADERSHIP FROM AN EXCEPTIONAL ROLE MODEL

"It's been my very great privilege to get to know Peter as a human being. So few of us in corporate America get that chance on a super deep level. It's truly a gift."

⤝

B Y LATE 2004, Kevin Jordan was ready for a career change. He had worked at Kaiser Permanente's Oakland, California, headquarters since 1998. After providing internal consulting and operations support for Kaiser's medical group, he joined a national project team to implement the privacy aspects of the 1996 Health Insurance Portability and Accountability Act (HIPAA). Kevin found that once his role morphed into a compliance function, "it wasn't very interesting or dynamic."

So, in early 2005, after returning from paternity leave for his daughter's birth, Kevin applied for a job as Operations Program Manager in the Internet Services Group (ISG). The position had remained unfilled for six months and would report to Peter Richter, who was then Senior Manager of ISG Operations.

Kevin explained, "This was the business side of kp.org serving Kaiser members, which was then only the website. We didn't yet have a mobile presence. We were part of marketing – a new field to me. I was interested in the role because it was a new, national function doing something that had never existed before. Many things were appealing, including the role's scalability and the opportunity to make a big impact. And, Peter had a strong reputation, especially when it came to growing people. I was excited because I had been stagnating in my compliance role."

Little did Kevin know what it would mean to work for Peter, but he got a hint of this during the job interview. "I told him that I was pretty excited about the role, but that I didn't know half of what was required," he admitted to Peter. According to Kevin, his prospective new manager responded, "I hire for two 'As' – aptitude and attitude. You have a great attitude, which means you're willing to learn and grow. I can teach you. And, you've demonstrated great aptitude for other parts of this job. You have a compliance background, an enterprise perspective, and an understanding of working with our regional partners. Your references are outstanding. So, I assume you have the potential to do this. It's a new role, and I haven't figured it all out either."

Aiming for His Manager's Job

The final interview question would prove to be significant in Kevin's Kaiser career. Peter asked him where he saw himself in five years. Kevin decided to have a little fun with his answer and replied that he wanted to be a director and to have Peter's job. At the time, Peter wasn't yet a director. Nevertheless, he reacted to Kevin's answer by smiling ear to ear and exclaiming, "OK, great!"

So, Kevin accepted Peter's job offer. But, his decision wasn't instantaneous. He learned that he'd have to take a lesser title at a lower pay grade than his compliance role. Peter explained that he could offer a bit more money, but that he had no flexibility with the title and pay grade. The prospect of moving backwards and the loss of a bonus opportunity gave Kevin pause, so he told Peter that he'd think about the offer overnight. Kevin recalled, "I went home to discuss the offer and its implications with my wife. I decided to accept Peter's offer, and it turned out to be the right move. Within six months, Peter promoted me back to my previous pay grade, and I just took off from there."

He described his first day on the job. "Peter, who was based in Denver at that time, had flown into Oakland. We sat down in a conference room, and he launched into his onboarding protocol – his values, ethics, expectations, goals, etc. Then he said, 'You want my job in five years. We're going to do it. I'm going to tee up the opportunity, and you're going to do it.' I was floored. No one had ever done anything like that with me – talk about development, opportunity, the next step. And, we ended up doing it in four and a half years."

He continued, "When I saw that Peter was confident enough to develop me for a role that he didn't yet have himself, that was corporate magic."

Getting to Know Peter

Kevin was in for many more delightful surprises as he got to know Peter. His new boss had grown up in Connecticut, graduated from Boston College, and completed a dual master's program in business administration and health administration at the University of Colorado in Denver. Peter had been working in ISG for a few years when Kevin joined his small team.

"He was smart and high energy, a fast talker, strategic thinker, and he quickly connected the dots. A deeply caring person, Peter had an abiding interest in people, was a great communicator and collaborator, always asking how he could help. He was all about the work and the people, not the drama and power plays. Very non-judgmental, Peter could work across all different types of groups," Kevin recalled.

His manager's collaborative leadership style was evident just four days into Kevin's new job. Peter had arranged a printout of a PowerPoint slide presentation on a conference table, told Kevin that he was stepping away for 15 minutes, and asked Kevin to review the material and comment on whether the story arc made sense the way the slides were ordered. Kevin recounted, "Peter assured me that he would take no offense if I pushed back or changed the order. No one had ever asked me to do something like that, let alone my boss. At first, I wondered if he was setting a trap, but he actually took many of my suggestions!"

Kevin explained that Peter was also known for his playful sense of humor. "If you forgot to lock your instant messaging account when you left your desk, Peter would walk by and send messages to people as if they were from you. He never sent anything offensive, but he did this to teach us to always lock our workstations because it was a compliance issue. He was a practical joker with a message who gauged his humor to his audience."

Learning Peter's Way

As they worked together, Peter gradually began mentoring Kevin, "a role that organically evolved over time." The learning started with the content of Kevin's new job – release management from the perspective of information technology (IT) and the organization it supported. He recalled the early days. "I had to learn the IT lingo and the basics of my role. And, I had to do this by becoming very self-sufficient because I was in Oakland, and Peter was in Denver. He assigned a buddy, and that's how I learned at first because he went on vacation for three weeks shortly after I started."

While Kevin honed his communication and collaboration skills, he quickly became Peter's eyes and ears on the ground in Oakland working with various teams. He credited his mentor with giving him "opportunities and visibility by virtue of Peter not being in Oakland much of the time."

An essential organizational skill that Peter taught Kevin was building alignment in a large, matrixed organization. Kevin would regularly shadow Peter at meetings to observe and learn. He recalled, "After these meetings, Peter would quiz me with lots of questions: 'What did you see happen? What was the body language? What didn't happen? Why do you think that person is happy?' It was almost the Socratic method of teaching in a polite, friendly way. I really honed my game because he pushed me to think in three, four, five dimensions."

One of the dimensions that Peter highlighted was "the meeting within the meeting." He would guide Kevin to pay attention to what was taking place on instant messaging while the live meeting was unfolding. Kevin elaborated, "Peter always stressed the importance of being aware of side meetings and their subtext. I learned to be more present and attuned to that."

Lessons in consensus building included techniques for selling Kevin's ideas to others. Peter would say to Kevin, "You're always selling something, and the organization needs to be ready to buy. Your ideas are great, but your timing sometimes sucks!" Then, Peter would flash one of his huge smiles. Kevin's mentor would guide him in strategic positioning by asking, "What would a successful pitch look like? How would the audience respond? Who needs to be brought along earlier rather than later? Who's an easy sell? Who's a hard sell?"

Facing New Challenges

Kevin's learning from Peter was characterized by his mentor's relentless push to challenge his mentee. He recalled Peter asking, "Are you ready to be uncomfortable?" Kevin elaborated, "When I did something well, and he was ready to promote me to the next level, he would tell me that I had to get uncomfortable again because the next level would be new and different. Peter would design my professional development goals to include experiences and stretch opportunities to grow. He helped me connect the dots, and he really set me up for success."

Kevin shared a story about a surprising challenge that

took place after Peter moved to Oakland. At first, they sat near each other on the same floor. One day, Peter announced that he was moving his office across the floor from Kevin, who initially questioned the decision. "But, then I realized Peter was doing that because, even at a super tactical level, he wanted to keep pushing me to grow. He was forcing me to take time to think things through before crossing the floor to get his input," he recalled.

Seeing the Bigger Picture

Connecting the dots to see the bigger picture was the framework from which Peter operated. This played out in multiple ways. According to Kevin, Peter taught him the value of always questioning rather than taking things at face value, which helped Kevin identify unspoken organizational needs that created opportunities for him.

The big picture also meant focusing beyond oneself to take care of partners, peers, and colleagues and to cover for team members. Kevin explained, "Our operations team was so great because we all just pitched in. There was a sense of selflessness. Peter set that tone. We knew we were part of something larger – the Kaiser mission, so it was our honor and obligation to serve our members. Peter carried that through our team meetings and his work. It is the core of who he is. We would ask ourselves, 'How do we create the best digital experience so our members can get their care?'"

Kevin reflected on how Peter came by the leadership wisdom that he imparted to others. "He was a serial student and avid learner who took advantage of Kaiser's management and leadership courses. He cultivated mentors inside and outside Kaiser, worked with professional coaches, and was open to experimenting with ideas from a diverse set of peers, partners, and direct reports. Peter did not seek credit. He sought to understand before being understood."

Building Their Relationship on Trust

Trust was the foundation of the relationship between Kevin and Peter. "Since nuance and subtlety can distort a message, we developed a very direct style. We could be open, honest, and transparent, but we never took it personally. Obviously, we did this behind closed doors, and we never offended each other. But, we could push each other hard if we had to. We gave each other the space to do that in a non-judgmental way. That was a huge part of my development, and it was a great gift," Kevin reminisced.

He continued, "In addition to being brutally honest with each other, we laughed a lot. We had fun. And, we would regularly debrief over lunch or dinner to unpack work. That's where Peter's use of the Socratic method often took place. We were getting to know each other in a different context."

The two of them were able to effectively represent each other so well that their colleagues would sometimes refer to them by each other's name. Kevin found this especially amusing because they physically look appreciably different from one another.

Their deepening relationship naturally evolved into friendship and sharing more of their personal lives with each other. Some of this took place during business trips, when they would inevitably run out of work-related topics of conversation. "We got to understand each other as people. And, we were judicious with that. Peter made sure that boundaries were pretty solid. He taught me how to have healthy work relationships, but to also be really good friends with someone at work, even your boss," Kevin observed.

Continuing His Career Journey

Their relationship took on a different dimension when Kevin was promoted to Director of Operations in 2010. That happened because Peter's portfolio of work kept growing, and the size of Kevin's portfolio was large enough to warrant the director title. So, they became peers on the same leadership team. Kevin recalled, "This restructuring kicked the mentor relationship into overdrive. Peter was still planning to help me on the side, and he gave me the space to establish myself at this level. He went well above and beyond what our boss expected in terms of transitioning me into my new role. Peter really welcomed me when I joined the leadership team. He helped me find my way and navigate the room at meetings because you don't know what you don't know when you join a new team."

In 2013, a pivotal career event for Kevin occurred when the department vice president retired. Another member of the leadership team became the interim manager for the balance of the year. During that year, Kevin and Peter had adjoining offices, and they leveraged their past relationship to work closely together. Kevin even managed one of Peter's teams for part of the year, although he wasn't accountable for the team.

After the arrival of the new department vice president in early 2014, some leadership team roles were renegotiated, others were transitioned, and the group as a whole moved in a new, strategic direction. Kevin recounted the chain of events. "My role was transitioned to another peer, and I was left at a bit of a crossroad without a natural or obvious professional home base in our evolving department. Peter and I had been discussing the evolution of our group and my future role in it. We explored the possibility of me working for him again and what that opportunity might look like. At the time, it was the next best fit for me, so in September 2014, I joined his team. While I loved working for Peter again, after a time, I realized that my heart was just not in the role or work required. It wasn't the best fit for my strengths and experience. So, I decided to move on."

Kevin described the June 2015 meeting when he broke the news to Peter. "We had been doing the dance of plausible deniability. I knew that Peter knew I was looking for work, but I didn't want to tell him in case our boss asked. I didn't want to put him in that position. One day, I told him I was coming into the office to chat. He walked into the conference room smiling and said, 'OK, so where are you going?' I told him that I just couldn't do the role anymore and that I had accepted a position heading up a program management office for a boutique consulting firm. We parted on exceptionally good terms. He was very gracious and understanding. I could not have asked for a better send-off."

But, Kevin's consulting job only lasted until September 2016, when he was laid off. He returned to Kaiser in the national human resources (HR) function in January 2017. At that point, Peter was Senior Director of Digital Planning, and he continued to mentor Kevin even though they worked in different groups. Then, in March 2019, Kevin was laid off from his HR role.

Evolving into His Calling

But, Kevin's second layoff was the catalyst for him to fully evolve into his coaching calling. His natural talent for coaching people had been emerging over time under Peter's mentorship. Kevin described his evolutionary journey. "When I worked for Peter, I realized that I wanted to learn how to manage people. I started mentoring students, contractors, and my own team. Peter helped me secure significant leadership development training opportunities. I began mentoring and coaching my peers' direct reports informally – and usually at their request. This was not part of my day-to-day responsibilities, but that did not matter to me; I thoroughly enjoyed the experiences." This activity spread into other parts of the organization as Kevin became a formal mentor in Kaiser's national program. Then, around 2013, he started doing private coaching outside Kaiser about 8-10 hours a week before and after work. "I did this not for the extra money, but because I loved it," he observed.

So, when Kevin was laid off in March 2019, he took a leap of faith and expanded full-time into his own executive, leadership, and career transformation coaching practice. Today he also provides consulting, meeting facilitation, and training services. His successful, blended practice includes his own private clients as well as subcontract work from other coaching and consulting firms.

Peter has even been one of Kevin's clients. He explained, "Peter hired me to strategize on organization development/ organization effectiveness opportunities for his team. He later told me that our time together had been foundational in terms of how he thought about the structure and design of his team."

Acknowledging Peter's Impact on His Career

Looking back on the entirety of his professional experiences with Peter, Kevin had a lot to say. "Without Peter, I would not have structured my Kaiser career the way I did or thought about it in multiple dimensions. He helped me look for opportunities to create and think about things holistically. His organization development/organization effectiveness mindset was unbelievably refreshing. I had assumed that other Kaiser employees were also getting that from their managers. Then, I looked around and realized that they weren't. I counted my blessings even more."

Kevin expressed his gratitude for the time that Peter spent and the risks he took to "give me stretch opportunities and let me fail in a safe but stretch way." He continued, "The amount of leadership training that I got in 10 years was just phenomenal. I didn't get anything like that before or after him. The people management experience I got at ISG was fundamental to becoming a coach. I learned the basics of management, then advanced to leadership, and evolved into organization development/organization effectiveness without being a practitioner in that field. I had a huge network of people available to teach, and Peter was the catalyst."

Kevin commented that he works with clients today "who don't have one tenth of what I got from Peter, and they're struggling as a result. I never took it for granted."

Carving Out a Post-Kaiser Relationship

"Now our relationship is purely a friendship. We still occasionally talk shop, and we sometimes mentor each other. Work was the base point of our relationship, but it hasn't defined us or been hugely instrumental in our lives for several years now. It's more part of our historical architecture than anything else. We've been able to carve out a relationship after Kaiser," Kevin reflected.

He concluded, "I've met Peter's mom and have been to his house in Connecticut. I know his partner. I'm part of his life to a degree. It's been my very great privilege to get to know Peter as a human being. So few of us in corporate America get that chance on a super deep level. It's truly a gift."

CHAPTER 9

BECOMING A HISTORIAN

"I learned from Bill and Jackie that being a historian is not something you do. It's something you are. I cannot ever operate in this world without thinking about origins of things."

⁓

DONNA SINCLAIR ENVISIONED much more for her life than waiting tables. As a child she loved learning and set her sights on teaching public school. But, she had a long road ahead. In 1992 – just after completing her associate degree from Clark College in Vancouver, Washington – her husband left her with three children ages 3, 4, and 8.

Donna waitressed wherever her husband had been posted in the Army. "My mother owned a restaurant when I was a girl, so I knew the business. At a Denny's in upstate New York, I waited tables, was head waitress, and wrote a training manual. I could have made more money in tips, but instead I chose to partly work off the floor to do the scheduling, training, and write the manual," she recalled. Perhaps it was an early indication of her yearning to share knowledge with others.

As a newly single mother, Donna juggled waitressing at a local Sizzler for $15 an hour and started classes at Washington State University Vancouver (WSUV) in fall 1993 – with help from the Pell Grant Program and student loans. She described the painful memories. "I was devastated. It was a horrible period of time. I was getting child support for three small children without much money. I was really lonely. It was very hard."

Having Epiphanies about History

WSUV would open doors and lay a career path for Donna in ways she couldn't imagine when she stepped into her first class. She had signed up for *Pacific Northwest History* taught by Dr. Bill Lang. She had no idea that meeting him was the start of a now 26-year relationship. Nor did she know the influence he would have on her career by "providing every professional opportunity and recommending me for jobs for 10 to 15 years."

"I remember being in a bad place emotionally that first day of class. Then I heard Bill talk about Native and non-Native concepts of time. I looked out the window as he was talking, and I started having a lot of epiphanies about change over time, contingencies, and the role of history in understanding human experience. I had always loved history and knew I would major in it, but I had no idea then that I would make a career out of it. Bill was a brilliant, erudite lecturer and introduced me to different ways of thinking about the past. I loved his class," she reminisced.

Donna continued, "He was the first person I ever heard talk about how historians work, pulling together remnants of the past into a coherent narrative. He likened historians' work to having someone in an airplane flying overhead rip up a newspaper and drop the pieces below. Historians have to put all the pieces together." Bill taught her about primary sources. And, his class helped her better understand her Pacific Northwest origins.

Discovering Public and Oral History

Donna also took *The American Frontier* and *Environmental History* with Bill. In one of these classes, he mentioned public history. She had never heard of it, so she asked him to explain more after class. He described it as a way to make ivory tower history palatable to the public, such as through museums, historic journals, public lectures, and historic sites like the National Park Service in Vancouver.

In those early days, Bill encouraged Donna to talk to another WSUV history professor, Dr. Jacqueline ("Jackie") Peterson, to learn about women missionaries. This was back in the day when WSUV had just a few history professors and 1,000 students at Baird Hall on Vancouver's Clark College campus. "It was a small community of professors and students, so we really got to know one another," Donna recalled.

Jackie already had a national reputation based on a major exhibit she had created, *Sacred Encounters*, about Native Americans and Catholics. So, meeting her would be another career milestone. Donna ended up taking public history classes with Jackie, which exposed her to a wide range of activities. Through these classes, she first learned about oral history – interviewing people about their own experiences of past events and ways of life to document history for the future.

Donna did her senior seminar in 1996 with Jackie. Her primary source research paper was on African Americans at Vanport City, Oregon, one of the nation's largest U.S. public housing projects during World War II. She had wondered why regional African Americans lived primarily in North Portland. Her research into Vanport revealed the large-scale migration of Blacks to Portland during the war and how the public housing project north of the city transitioned into a low-income, veterans, and "Negro project" after the war. She also learned about the massive Columbia River flood that wiped out Vanport City on May 30, 1948, and how the local Red Cross started a chain of segregation during flood relief that located the Black community in North Portland.

She described Jackie as a professor. "Having entered the profession in the late 60s, she operated in a very authoritative manner. Jackie was tough in that class. She didn't tolerate any fools and could be hard on students. But, I did well, and Jackie liked me. She helped me become a better writer."

But, even before her senior seminar, Jackie had started taking Donna under her wing. In 1995, Donna was working as a WSUV program assistant when Jackie hired her to help plan a Portland conference for the American Society for Environmental History. The conference was scheduled to take place the following year. "She took me places with her. We attended meetings together, like with hotel staff to negotiate the conference contract. I had numerous opportunities to listen and learn. Jackie even took me with her to a Pacific Northwest History conference in Seattle and paid for me to attend my first oral history workshop. I met several oral historians there whom I later came to know quite well. These were experiences that I didn't know existed. I was learning about a profession."

Donna also worked for Jackie on her *Women in the West* oral history project. This gave her a hands-on opportunity to listen to recorded interviews while ensuring transcription accuracy, then cataloguing them.

Identifying Role Models as Mentors

Bill and Jackie were both superb role models with impressive credentials, and Donna came to think of them as her mentors.

Bill's specialties included environmental, public, social, Western, and Native American history. Donna characterized him as a deal maker because "he always had about 10 different activities going on, making things happen. He would match people with jobs and programs with opportunities." He had previously been editor of *Montana Magazine*. In 1991, Bill put together a nonprofit consortium, the Center for Columbia River History (CCRH), in partnership with the Washington State Historical Society, WSUV, and Portland State University (PSU). This was the realization of Bill's vision for bridging the gap between academia and public history.

Donna attributed Bill's deal making talent to his interpersonal skills. She recalled, "He could talk to anybody – loggers in the woods or people in high, public offices. He was kind, gentle, caring, and extremely generous with his time." She shared a warm memory of him stopping by her home when she was snowbound without childcare to pick up a school paper that was due. Years later, when she became a Ph.D. candidate, he readily agreed to sit on her dissertation committee.

It was easy for Donna to learn from Bill because they both thought "in a circular, complex way." She explained, "My mind clicked with his. He taught me how to think deeply. He would say, 'Watch the bouncing ball. Where does it take you? What's at the root?'" Bill meant that historians have to piece together stories in meaningful ways.

Donna described Jackie as "scary brilliant." One of the few women scholars of Native American history, Jackie had once worked at the prestigious Newberry Library in Chicago, which housed important archives. "She knew the major U.S. figures in Native history and had a prominent, Native American history scholar as her own mentor," Donna recalled.

A tiny woman, Jackie was "fierce" according to Donna, who shared memories of her talking fast and moving fast. "You could hear Jackie marching through the halls. She was hardly ever in her office and often came rushing into class late. Then, when she arrived, rather than being flustered, she was brilliant without lecture notes. She knew everything. I loved her as a teacher then and later as a human being."

Like Bill, Jackie knew how to get things done. Donna remembered that she "never took 'no' for an answer, yet she could be quite charming." Jackie's fierceness was balanced by her generosity and warmth. She would throw parties for students in her public history class and hosted a graduation party for Donna when she eventually completed her Ph.D. many years later.

Pivoting Her Career Choice

By the time she graduated from WSUV in 1996 with a Bachelor of Science in history and a minor in anthropology, Donna had chosen public history as her career goal. "I decided not to go into teaching public school, so I applied for and was accepted into a master's program at PSU in environmental and cultural history. If it hadn't been for Bill and Jackie, I would probably have become a public school teacher," Donna observed.

There was just one problem. Donna had taken out $20,000 in student loans to attend WSUV and had no money for graduate school. After graduation, she was working in the WSUV Education Department and for Jackie at the 1996 American Society for Environmental History Conference. She had only recently stopped waitressing at Sizzler.

Then, Donna ran into Bill at the conference. He had left WSUV, was on a tenured faculty track at PSU, and CCRH had been underway since 1991. "I hadn't seen him in a year. He gave me a big hug and said he was excited that I had chosen public history," Donna recalled. Not long after that, Bill called her at the WSUV Education Department and asked if she still wanted to go to graduate school. He had found money to fund her master's degree through a CCRH endowment.

That's when Bill told Donna that she was the best student he had ever had. "A good mentor helps you see your strengths. Bill once commented on one of my papers that I had a 'talent for the ironic.' I didn't realize before then that I had any sort of talent," Donna recalled.

Learning Public History Outside the Classroom

She started her master's program at PSU in the winter of 1997, and Bill was one of her main professors. He also hired her to work as a CCRH research assistant. "The classes themselves were background to my CCRH apprenticeship," she explained. Donna was earning $300 a month and received tuition remission for working 15 hours a week. She still had to take out another $20,000 in student loans.

When Bill got a $300,000 grant from the U.S. Department of Education the following year, it opened up new opportunities for Donna. He offered her three options – working in the Oral History Department for the Oregon Historical Society, helping with a curriculum project, or building the brand new CCRH website. She chose the website and created online exhibits, which required learning html when it was new, doing oral history, and conducting field research in communities.

By this time, Donna had become the WSUV resident historical transcriptionist for $8 an hour – a role that Jackie helped her land. This was in addition to attending PSU classes and working for Bill at CCRH. She recalled doing "a bunch of transcription projects at WSUV, such as on homeless women, World War II vets, an Arikara language project, and Indian women becoming dental assistants."

But, she still struggled to make ends meet. So, through Bill, Donna accepted a grant-funded conservation project at the Oregon Historical Society. She transferred the sound from aluminum and glass recordings (78 RPM records) onto audio tape cassettes and catalogued them. These World War II era records had been used for radio programs. They held local recordings on one side and national programs like

President Roosevelt's fireside chats on the other. "It was like living through World War II," Donna explained.

Gaining Visibility

She recalled more opportunities that Bill created for her. "One of my early paid history jobs occurred when Bill asked me to write a report on the Nez Perce Indians for the Washington State Historical Society (WSHS). Thirty-three men, women, and children from the Red Heart Band had been incarcerated at Vancouver Barracks from August 1877 until April 22, 1878, during the Nez Perce War. I did original research that documented their imprisonment and the date of their release, resulting in a reconciliation ceremony on April 22, 1998, in partnership with WSHS, the City of Vancouver, and the Nez Perce Tribe. This historic event has been commemorated in Vancouver every April since then. And, I wrote my first published article based on the report. I even won an award for it." Donna was gaining visibility in her new field.

In 2000, Bill arranged another deal that led to a four-year, prestigious role for Donna. A major West Coast oral history program at the Oregon Historical Society was at risk of ending around the time the director was retiring. There had been accusations that the program only recorded vanity interviews of influential people rather than those whose voices had gone undocumented, such as women and people of color.

Determined to save the program, Bill became an ex officio member of the regional oral historian advisory board. In this capacity, he made it possible for Donna to work 21.75 hours a week (while continuing her work at CCRH) directing the program and simultaneously conducting an evaluation.

Donna soon discovered that the funding model was a problem because it relied on corporate and vanity interviews, not the collection itself. "In my final evaluation report, I recommended that the program should not have to exist on grant funds or contracts, but should have operational funds," she recounted. The advisory board agreed. Her report also highlighted the value of interviews with legislators from eastern Oregon ranches, lawyers who had been soldiers in World War II, women who had worked in the shipyards, and African Americans from Vanport. The collection was an amazing resource, but it needed more diversity. Stable funding would make that possible.

Donna continued as director until 2004 (the year she completed her master's degree at PSU), when the program was suspended after state budget cuts hit the historical society hard. But, the experience that she gained in those four years was invaluable. She explained, "I had heard the prior program director speak when I was a student, and I'd wished I could have his job someday. I never thought that I'd ever actually get it! The Oregon Historical Society is top tier, and serving as director of the oral history program set me on a path to becoming an independent, oral history consultant."

New experiences kept materializing for Donna under Bill's mentorship. Because she had served as director of the Oregon Historical Society oral history program, she was able to take a contract with the U.S. District Court of the Oregon Historical Society from 2004 to 2008. The Arlington Club, a prestigious social club for Portland business people, also hired her to do oral histories and ultimately write a book about the club's history, *Arlington Club: Where Leaders Meet*.

Opening New Doors and Closing Others

Meanwhile in 2005, Donna set out to achieve a new career goal. She applied and was accepted into the PSU Ph.D. program in urban studies – a degree that she ultimately completed 10 years later while continuing to build her reputation as a public historian. She worked there with a well-known urban historian, Dr. Carl Abbott, who allowed her to marry the issues that mattered to her – gender, race, representation, and environment through a dissertation that explored intersections of federal policy and individual experience.

Her dissertation, "Caring for the Land, Serving People: the US Forest Service in the Civil Rights Era," uses oral history interviews and documents to examine how a white, male federal agency brought women and people of color into its workforce. This part of her education was partially funded by the PSU adjunct faculty association and through another stint at CCRH, which provided additional tuition remission. A 2013 Catherine Prelinger Award of $20,000 for non-traditional female historians helped her finish the work and make possible her degree completion without additional loans. "I'd have never taken on a Ph.D. without the financial assistance," she said.

Continuing as a PSU adjunct history professor, Donna returned to CCRH in 2008 and became program manager, a role she had coveted eight years earlier before completing her master's degree. But, CCRH was in its final years. She recalled, "The program was incrementally diminished from full-time to one day a week because the Washington State Historical Society lost funding. I started as program manager the year the stock market crashed, which impacted funding.

The program ended in 2012 after a good, 21-year run. It was very sad. I actually packed the boxes and closed up the organization all by myself. My professional life has its roots in that time period."

Developing a Career Perspective

Donna gave enormous credit to Bill and Jackie not only for the doors they opened, but also for teaching her things that shaped her career perspective.

They emphasized that writing was essential to her success, and both mentors helped her hone this critical skill. "I learned to write from Bill, and Jackie taught me the importance of chronology," she commented.

"Bill showed me that I was capable of things I didn't know I could do. He once said that he just put me out there, and I was the one who did the work. He knew I'd work hard enough to make things happen. I learned that I could figure it out as I went."

She continued, "He gave me professional confidence in my talents, such as being a people person, which proved invaluable as a public historian. He even showed me how I could apply my waitressing skills, like multi-tasking and business knowledge, to history. And, because of him, I learned to walk into a room full of high-level professionals knowing I was as good as any of them."

Jackie modeled being fierce and simultaneously respected as a woman. Donna elaborated, "Fortunately, I didn't have to adopt some of the more forceful traits that Jackie had developed because I was a generation behind her. She taught me that community activity really matters. For example,

Jackie had single-handedly brought an organization to life in Portland's Chinatown. I also learned from her how to interact with indigenous people by really listening to them."

Both of Donna's mentors modeled doing meaningful work and fulfilling intellectual passions at the same time. And, most important of all, Donna said she "learned from Bill and Jackie that being a historian is not something you do. It's something you are. I cannot ever operate in this world without thinking about origins of things."

Enjoying Lifelong Friendships

Over the years, Donna's relationships with Bill and Jackie evolved into friendships.

She explained, "Bill became a lot like a father figure, and he is a friend. He would always stop whatever he was doing when I came by his office. He took an interest in my kids. He came to our wedding for my second marriage. He and his wife, Marianne, have invited us to dinner in their home. We exchange Christmas letters. I know his stepdaughter."

"The same is true for Jackie. She's been a wonderful, incredibly generous friend and has even given me things like bookshelves and paintings. She's an amazing person. I know I could always reach out to her if I needed something," Donna added.

Researching, Writing, Teaching, and Serving

Dr. Donna Sinclair has become a well-established, independent, public history consultant devoted to research, writing, and editing. She has also continued teaching at PSU, Western Oregon University, and WSUV – where she joined the adjunct faculty in 2011 at the prompting of Dr. Sue Peabody. "Sue and Dr. Laurie Mercier also served as important female historian role models during my earlier association with WSUV and CCRH. I can't thank them enough for showing me that women can be historians too," Donna commented.

In addition, she has written extensively for the National Park Service, has a published oral history collection, a chapter in *Reshaping Women's History: Voices of Non-traditional Women Historians,* and has co-written a memoir with the first African American female forest supervisor in the country. *Black Woman in Green: Gloria Brown and the Unmarked Trail to Forest Service Leadership* was published in February 2020 by Oregon State University Press.

As of this writing, she also serves on the Washougal, Washington, School Board of Directors and is running for a seat in the Washington State House of Representatives. Leveraging her public history work, Donna regards politics as the natural next step in her career evolution.

Perhaps most significant is that Donna has become a role model for young students. She reflected, "The circle of mentoring is really important for those who come behind us. I've learned from others, so now if I have a student who needs an extra leg up, I will help. Many of my students come from working class backgrounds like I did. I guide them along by telling them how things work and providing opportunities. I share my own experiences to encourage them. I advise them to follow their passions. But, I also say they may not make very much money in the field of public history, so if security is important to them, they need to know that about themselves."

Donna is passing on the legacy that she inherited from

Bill and Jackie. She hasn't waited tables in many years. Instead, she's serving a rich history menu to the public and her students. And, for her students, life lessons are dessert.

Chapter 10

Developing His Own
Handwriting

*"I value movement as much as stillness. Feldenkrais work
recognizes in a deeper way that mind and body are not
separate. You get a whole different level of awareness by
paying attention to movement, which is itself a meditation."*

❧

RUSSELL DELMAN WAS steeped in the San
Francisco Human Potential Movement in the early
1970s. "It was already clear from age 18 that I would
be some sort of teacher on a path toward awareness. The
whole Human Potential thing was in my bones very early,"
he recalled. After graduating at age 20 from Pennsylvania's
Lehigh University with a Bachelor of Arts in psychology and
magna cum laude honors, he returned to the Bay Area, where
he started teaching yoga and leading meditation groups.

The only "real job with a paycheck" that Russell ever had
was working in a drug rehabilitation center, which he did for
one year. Mostly he was "just making ends meet" through his

yoga and meditation work. Russell started attending classes at the Esalen Institute in 1971. It was there that he first heard about Moshe Feldenkrais from a "good friend well known in the Human Potential Movement." His friend advised Russell, "If you ever get the chance to study with this guy, do it." Russell was intrigued by Feldenkrais' reputation for being "the leading edge of somatic learning – learning through the body."

Then, one day in 1975, he opened his mailbox to find a flier advertising Moshe Feldenkrais' first North American professional training program in San Francisco, conducted by the Humanistic Psychology Institute, for $5,000. Coincidentally, he had just inherited $5,000 from his mother, so Russell got his chance to study with the master.

When signing up for the Feldenkrais training, Russell was already five years into what would become a lifelong Zen meditation practice. He had also been studying and practicing various forms of somatic awareness. At that point, Russell didn't yet realize that the Feldenkrais teachings would deepen, expand, and transform these other practices into a profession. The eventual result years later would be his successful, international school of awareness, *The Embodied Life*.

Seeking a Pure Experience

Russell described the San Francisco scene 45 years ago as "a different time." He said, "We were hippies living in the Bay Area enjoying life, and hopefully we could earn enough money to make ends meet, but that was not the center of the calling. When I decided to study with Moshe, who eventually became my most significant mentor, it was in the far background that I was starting to grow a career."

He began his Feldenkrais studies when there were no practitioners in the country. Russell was on a pioneering journey. He described himself as an "anti-intellectual hippie at the time" who intentionally chose not to read about the Feldenkrais work before stepping into Moshe's classroom. He sought "a pure experience with no expectations and where every day would be a surprise." That was Russell's attitude when he showed up the first day in June 1975 at Lone Mountain College for the training.

Experiencing the Feldenkrais Method

And, he did encounter many surprises during the professional training. Moshe's teaching style consisted of putting his students through "lots of experiences" without much explanation and "encouraging us to come to our own meaning."

Russell described the two forms of the Feldenkrais Method, which he learned experientially. *Awareness through Movement* is a series of group lessons covering over 1,000 functional movement patterns. Feldenkrais had developed the lessons after having taught judo and devising new ways of moving to heal his own severe knee injuries.

"The slow, gentle, meditations of movement are designed to make clients more aware of their habits and develop new motor patterns as they work through the lesson instructions. Moshe really understood how the brain can grow new neural patterns, which is the purpose behind the lessons," he explained.

The second Feldenkrais form is *Functional Integration* – private, hands-on work between practitioner and client. According to Russell, this work is based on "the same idea of teaching your nervous system to learn new patterns by experiencing them."

A wide range of clients seek both forms of the Feldenkrais Method, such as athletes, dancers, singers, those who have suffered brain injuries, and individuals who have had physical therapy and desire further improvement.

"It's best known for the purpose of rehabilitation, kind of like advanced physical therapy. But, that's only part of the Feldenkrais work. Moshe's vision was to help humans become more aware of themselves by learning to pay attention to their movement. He clearly saw that our physical patterns are intimately connected to our emotional patterns and our thinking patterns because we are whole human beings. The way we hold our breath, stand, sit, and reach for things are expressions of us and how we relate to the world," Russell explained.

He added that Moshe believed making deep change requires addressing mental and emotional issues through physical patterns of movement, which are the "infrastructure for our mental and emotional stories." The Feldenkrais Method grew out of Moshe's passion for the inner life of meditation and belief that awareness is the next evolutionary stage of the human brain, according to Russell.

Developing Mind and Body

Russell described his mentor as "a Renaissance man of true genius who was intellectually brilliant, but also very much in his body." He shared some highlights of Moshe's dramatic life and the origins of his method.

Born into an orthodox Jewish family in the Ukraine in 1904, Moshe was an observant child and independent thinker who kept nature journals and read sophisticated psychology at age 12.

While he "wasn't particularly religious," according to Russell, both of his grandfathers were famous rabbis, and he was surrounded by Talmudic thought. With World War I underway, at age 13, Moshe was alarmed by the pogroms, in which countless Jews were being killed. So, in 1918, he made the life-changing decision to leave his family and travel cross-country with a group of villagers on foot and horseback to catch a boat to Haifa in Palestine.

He had many formative experiences during his teen and young adult years in Palestine. A strong, young athlete, Moshe learned jiu jitsu from a British colonel. As he gained proficiency in martial arts in his early 20s, he wrote his first two books – one on combat and another on judo. Also brilliant in mathematics, Moshe became a surveyor and made some of the first maps of his new home country.

During the 1930s, Moshe lived in Paris, where he graduated with an engineering degree from the Ecole Speciale des Travaux Publics and a Doctor of Science in physics from the University of Paris. Madame Marie Curie, who discovered radium and developed the theory of radioactivity, was one of his teachers.[13]

Although Moshe spoke six languages, French wasn't one of them when he initially studied for his engineering degree. Russell shared a story about his mentor's creative way of coping with the language barrier. "He was a really funny, clever guy. Moshe had picked up a French street sign that meant, "Go slow. Children present." He would sit in the

13 "Moshe Feldenkrais," Wikipedia. Accessed January 14, 2020.
https://en.wikipedia.org/wiki/Mosh%C3%A9_Feldenkrais.

back of the classroom and hold up the sign when he couldn't understand the teacher."

Studying engineering in French didn't stop Moshe from succeeding. Russell explained that his mentor "got passing grades in his first year, was in the top three of his class in the second year, and graduated at the top of his class with grades that were the most outstanding the school had ever seen."

While living in Paris, Moshe learned from an ambassador that the Japanese professor, Jigoro Kano, the inventor of modern judo, was planning to give a demonstration. Moshe brought the book he had written on judo to the event and shared it with Kano. Russell's mentor had developed a move to take a knife away from an attacker, and Kano responded that it was impossible. So, Kano asked his most famous judo practitioner to come at Moshe with a knife, and Moshe showed his opponent the move. "This is how he got his move into the judo curriculum. He was the first Caucasian to do that," Russell commented.

During these years, Moshe co-founded a judo school, taught the martial art at night, and worked at Madame Curie's laboratory, the Radium Institute, during the day. Her son-in-law, Frederic Joliot-Curie, was one of his judo students. And, Moshe was Frederic's research assistant in the lab. This was Moshe's life early in World War II when he learned that the Nazis were rapidly approaching Paris. So, in 1940, he escaped the French capital, carrying heavy water developed in the lab along with research notes. He delivered these items to the British Admiralty War Office in England.[14]

---

14 "Moshe Feldenkrais," Wikipedia. Accessed January 14, 2020.
https://en.wikipedia.org/wiki/Mosh%C3%A9_Feldenkrais.

Upon landing in England, Moshe was initially placed in "something like a concentration camp because the English weren't letting everyone in. But, a scientist cleared his name, and he then lived with a group of scientists in Scotland working on the war effort. It was the beginning of cybernetics (the comparative study of human control systems and complex electronic systems[15]). They were trying to predict invasion patterns that the Germans might use in England," Russell recounted.

Steering His Life in a New Direction

Another life-changing event took place when Moshe was working on a submarine in Scotland in the mid-1940s. He had already sustained a knee injury playing soccer in 1929. So, when he slipped and fell on the submarine, Moshe was unable to walk. He was told that he would need surgery, but he refused that treatment. Instead, Moshe applied everything he had learned from judo about moving more efficiently, taught himself to walk again, and avoided surgery. He gradually developed the Feldenkrais Method out of his self-rehabilitation process. This led to writing his first book on the Feldenkrais Method, *Body and Mature Behavior: A Study of Anxiety, Sex, Gravitation, and Learning,* which was published in 1949.

In 1951, Moshe returned to what had become the state of Israel in 1948.[16] Back in his home country, he started to be

---

15 *Webster's New World Dictionary, 3rd College Edition* (New York: Simon & Schuster, Inc., 1988), 343.

16 "Moshe Feldenkrais," Wikipedia. Accessed January 14, 2020. https://en.wikipedia.org/wiki/Mosh%C3%A9_Feldenkrais.

known for his Feldenkrais work and developed a relationship with David Ben-Gurion, Israel's first prime minister, as his personal trainer and friend.

Russell observed about this period in his mentor's timeline, "As he approached age 50, Moshe changed his life from science to expanding his Feldenkrais Method. It was a gradual process of leveraging all his life skills and some of his most important qualities."

Building a Personal Relationship

As Russell studied the Feldenkrais Method under Moshe, their mentor-mentee relationship slowly developed into a deep, personal connection over nine years. Russell recalled, "During the first three to four years, I was pretty intimidated. He was quite strong in self-expression, and I was very young. We were like grandfather and grandson, and I wanted his approval. I really didn't know if he saw me as an individual when I was in a class of 65 people. Only later did I realize that I was always someone special to him."

They stayed in contact despite the distance between San Francisco and Israel. Russell attended Moshe's public workshops in the United States. Then in 1979, an event took place that ultimately brought them closer together. Russell had a car accident while driving to the Humanistic Psychology Institute annual conference to deliver his first presentation on the Feldenkrais Method. He had broken some bones in his neck and reached out to his mentor, who was planning to deliver a seminar a few months later in Washington, D.C.

"I asked if I could get a session from him. Moshe suggested that I come to the seminar, and he would see if he could help my movement. In one of his lessons, I went from wearing a collar to being pain-free. Then, I hung out with him after the seminar in his hotel room. When we sat and talked, we started developing a more personal connection. And, later that year, I went to Israel with my wife and watched him work every day," Russell recalled.

Their relationship continued to blossom, and Russell started assisting in Moshe's classes in 1980 and 1981. Russell's wife attended one of the classes.

And, more events were yet to unfold that deepened their bond.

Observing from Multiple Points of View

One of Moshe's "most important qualities" as a mentor, according to Russell, was his practice of questioning everything, always taking a fresh perspective. He explained, "Moshe encouraged me to not go with the status quo, not believe other people's opinions or take on the culture's view of things, but to look at everything from three, four, or five points of view."

Russell experienced Moshe's delivery of such advice as "challenging" at times. "A lot of people didn't like working with him because he was very direct – argumentative and yelling a lot. You had to have a strong sense of yourself to be with him," he commented.

He told a story that illustrated his mentor's practice of looking at things from multiple points of view and Moshe's blunt communication style. The incident took place at a time that was a big leap forward in their mentor-mentee relationship. Moshe had a stroke in late 1981. So, in 1982, Russell flew to Israel to administer Feldenkrais lessons for Moshe's rehabilitation twice a day for three weeks. The two were together daily from morning until around 8 p.m.

Russell reminisced, "One day we were sitting at his desk when Moshe turned on the radio to hear the news at 12 noon. He would translate for me because I don't speak Hebrew. At this time, the Israeli Air Force was bombing Lebanon, and we could hear the planes flying overhead. I exclaimed to him, 'Oh, Moshe, when are human beings going to get to the point where they don't have to kill each other to solve their problems? This is ridiculous. These bombs are killing lots of people.' He looked at me and said, 'Russell, you're an idiot! Have you ever really thought that in the history of humanity, almost all medical research has come out of war, almost every great advancement in science is because of war? Have you ever thought the reason why there's genetic diversity is because of war? Have you ever realized that more cultures have intermingled and learned from each other because of war?'" And, Moshe continued on with more such declarations about the evolution of humanity due to war.

Russell walked back to his place that evening with his head spinning. He observed, "I had the very clear realization that, once I knew I was right about peace being good and war being bad, I had stopped thinking. That was Moshe's main message – to never stop thinking, but to keep looking from many points of view."

The next day, when Russell and Moshe again listened to the news at 12 noon, Russell commented, "Oh, isn't it great? They're saving humanity!" And, Moshe replied, "Russell, you're an idiot! What could be worse than killing innocent children?"

"He saw that paradox is closer to truth and that looking from many points of view is essential to get anywhere close to holistic understanding. He challenged me to always think freshly. It was part of his Talmudic background to question everything and argue another point of view. That was very different than the culture I lived in during the 60s and 70s," Russell explained.

Within the context of Moshe's intellectual challenges, Russell acknowledged how their relationship advanced at that time. He commented, "We grew even closer. I learned so much being with him during that three-week period when he was trying to get back to functioning, and we had to utilize his own work to help him."

Studying Diligently and Thinking Freely

As the learning process unfolded, Moshe urged Russell to adapt the Feldenkrais work. Russell explained, "One of Moshe's favorite expressions was 'you must develop your own handwriting. Don't just copy me. Your handwriting must be legible, but let it be your own.' The goal was to not strive to become Moshe, but rather to first learn well, then experience the freedom to improvise – be both diligent in your study and free in your thinking."

This mission of developing his own handwriting continued to play out during Russell's remaining time with Moshe – and beyond.

"Moshe was half-way through conducting his second, in-depth, professional training in 1983 when he had another stroke. He had his Israeli assistants complete the training with some of us Americans supporting them," Russell recalled. And, once again, the mentee traveled to Israel to administer Feldenkrais lessons to his beloved mentor.

Then Moshe developed a succession plan. "When he realized he wasn't going to be able to conduct training anymore, he selected about 10 people, including me, to become the first Feldenkrais professional trainers." The Feldenkrais Institute was created in 1984 to deliver such training at Dominican University in San Rafael, California.

Russell was busy leading a training class at the university when news arrived that Moshe had died on July 4, 1984. The last time he had seen his mentor in person was in September 1983. "It was shocking because I didn't realize he was declining so quickly," Russell recalled. The Feldenkrais Institute community members held a memorial ceremony for Moshe at the university.

And, the event was another milestone on Russell's handwriting journey. He commented, "There was actually something empowering about knowing that he really valued the way I had brought the work into the world, and that he was now gone. I was there to help carry it on."

Integrating the Feldenkrais Work After Moshe

Since Moshe's death, Russell has continued to evolve his own handwriting. He conducted professional training and offered *Awareness through Movement and Functional Integration* to clients for many years. He explained, "I developed a parallel path in the 1990s, *The Embodied Life* school, combining Zen meditation with ways of exploring our emotions and communicating, which was more holistic." Russell said that 10 years ago he "stopped doing standalone Feldenkrais work to focus exclusively on *The Embodied Life*." But, he expanded the program to integrate Feldenkrais.

Russell's *Embodied Life* seminars and residential retreats now include three components – embodied meditation, Feldenkrais movement lessons, and guided inquiry. The meditation component addresses being present "with the thoughts, feelings, and sensations that arise from moment to moment." The Feldenkrais movement lessons serve to "eliminate ineffective habits of standing, breathing, sitting, and walking as well as unconscious contractions due to stress reactions." And, the guided inquiry component "is a study of our physical/mental habits, belief structures, and relational and communication patterns."

Russell shared an important insight about the Feldenkrais contribution to *The Embodied Life*. He described the grounded, centered presence that derives from Feldenkrais work. "It's hard to imagine that physical embodiment could come only through the Zen meditation. I value movement as much as stillness. Feldenkrais work recognizes in a deeper way that mind and body are not separate. You get a whole different level of awareness by paying attention to movement, which is itself a meditation."

Based on this belief, Russell is concerned that Feldenkrais work in the world "is being turned into sophisticated physical therapy, and the awareness and transcendent aspects of the work are being lost." So, he strives to keep the true essence of Feldenkrais alive and well through his *Embodied Life* school. And, in staying true to his calling, Russell has built a fulfilling, lifelong career with the surprising side benefit of financial security.

Giving and Receiving Ongoing Guidance

As a professional Feldenkrais trainer and *Embodied Life* mentor, a central aspect of Russell's role has been guiding countless students in their personal and professional development. He commented on what he experienced about mentoring over the years from his role model. "Moshe was always just himself in the company of others and never put on airs. I have modeled being authentic and natural with everyone. And, as he did, I strive to honor my students' individuality and help them discover their 'own handwriting.' Finally, while valuing each person, Moshe did not support ego trips. I also point out unhelpful self-aggrandizement if I observe it in my students."

Russell's handwriting has indeed matured, yet he continues to receive inspiration from Moshe. He revealed that their relationship is inwardly "ongoing in the sense that I still talk to him, still look for guidance, and Moshe still lives in my heart and the background of my life."

CHAPTER 11

FINDING HER VOICE IN ACT 3

*"She helped me through a very difficult, transitional
time and got me on the right path. Then, she shoved me
out of the nest when our paths started to diverge."*

ي

"MY LIFE UP to age 35 was playing music all day long – work or go to school, come home and rehearse, perform, or listen to my friends perform. It was one big flow. Life was about sound and being in rhythm with others. It was difficult to imagine a life without this, both professionally and socially," Liz Williams reflected.

She had graduated from Michigan's Oakland University in 1980 with a Bachelor of Science in music education focusing on classical guitar. One year later, she became board certified in the music therapy program of Wayne State University, also in Michigan. This was after completing an internship at Sonoma State Hospital (now Sonoma Developmental Center) in northern California. Over the next five years, Liz assessed and treated developmentally and intellectually disabled adults at the same hospital. Through music, she was able to reach severely limited patients in ways they couldn't otherwise be reached. She also played bass guitar for residents in the hospital's house band and at state-wide hospital functions.

Other venues for Liz's musical performances included bars, cafes, craft fairs, private parties, and corporate events in the San Francisco Bay Area. While she cut her teeth on classical guitar, she had more opportunities to play electric and upright bass. Liz thrived on music.

Enduring Physical Injuries

Then she severely injured her back maneuvering a heavy patient out of a wheelchair and was forced to take a year off work. This incident ended Liz's music therapy career, which required optimal physical fitness to handle patients. After recovering enough to work again, she took an entry-level job at a San Francisco ad agency. Liz was being groomed to be general manager when she was laid off.

At that point, she ventured into a world that was totally foreign to her – corporate America. Liz accepted a technical writing position in the Information Technology (IT) department at Kaiser Permanente's Oakland, California, headquarters. During this time, she continued feeding her guitar passion playing at Bay Area venues. But, five years into her Kaiser job, typing from 9 to 5 and plucking guitar strings the rest of her waking hours had taken its toll. Liz was diagnosed with carpal tunnel syndrome and focal dystonia, a condition that "afflicts many string players where the fingers don't obey the brain." For the second time, a physical injury drove her to find a new career.

Having grown bored with technical writing, Liz was already half way through a master's program in adult education and group dynamics at San Francisco State University when her hands gave out. No longer able to play music and daunted by the realization that most careers required using her hands, she sunk into deep depression for years. "I had to figure out how to make a living using my voice," Liz recalled.

Listening to Life-Changing Advice

But, serendipity offered a turning point in her life. At her last class before Liz paused her master's program due to her latest injury, her teacher told her about a nine-month internship in Kaiser's organization development (OD) group. In those days, it was called Consulting, Research, and Development (CRD). Liz observed, "It was one of those life moments when I just knew I should listen to her." But, she had serious reservations because she hadn't yet completed her master's degree – one of the internship requirements – and her hands didn't work. "This was on a Thursday, and the application was due the following Monday. The application process required a boatload of stuff, so I took a lot of Ibuprofen and went for it. I spent the weekend typing up the materials and delivered them at 5 p.m. on Monday," she recalled.

Without a master's degree (which she eventually completed in 1996), Liz landed the half-time internship in the training department (the "Development" side of CRD) in 1992. She didn't yet realize that she was stepping into a life-changing, third act career under the mentorship of Jean Westcott. The relationship would last for nine years.

According to Liz, "Jean was the queen of meetings and meeting skills, and she always coached the interns." Her new mentor, 14 years older, functioned as a trainer, although she reported into the "Consulting and Research" side of CRD. This was Liz's introduction to the corporate training field, where she would gradually develop her professional voice as a talented trainer, meeting facilitator, and consultant.

Meeting OD Leaders

"Jean was as non-corporate as they come. In the early days of OD, this was typical. It was an asset, and it came out of the hippie era," Liz explained.

Jean had graduated from the renowned University of Massachusetts OD program with a doctoral degree. Her own advisor had been leadership guru Ken Blanchard, best known for his situational leadership model and the book, *The One Minute Manager*. Another of Jean's mentors was cross-cultural anthropologist, Angeles Arrien, author of *Four-Fold Way: Walking the Paths of the Warrior, Healer, Teacher and Visionary*.

She ran in first generation OD circles when T-groups – sensitivity training groups for interpersonal insights – were all the rage. Jean had participated in the very first T-group on the West Coast. Many of her UMass OD colleagues had also moved to the West Coast, and Jean stayed connected to them.

Immersed in this high-powered OD world, Jean gave Liz an entree into that generation. "It was intimidating to be around people older and more accomplished. I was learning a new field, and my hands didn't work. I couldn't even shake hands when I met these influential people," Liz reflected.

Speaking Truth to Power

But, Liz wasn't intimidated by Jean herself. She found her mentor to be "fun, mischievous, playful, authentic, and a truth teller." Liz was fascinated by Jean's ease with speaking truth to power – a foundational lesson in her early corporate career. Liz shared two favorite stories about her mentor's talent for wielding personal power with executives.

One day the Kaiser CEO had asked Jean to facilitate some meetings for him. Jean didn't hold back in expressing serious reservations. She told the CEO that C-level executives typically abused her time by expecting her to be available anytime, anywhere. She added that these executives often showed up unprepared. The CEO responded that her concerns were fair, and they made an agreement. Jean insisted on no calls after 5 p.m. and requested direct access to him, not through his assistant. "She drove a hard bargain, and he agreed to it," Liz recounted.

On another occasion, Jean was in a meeting where an executive was denigrating consultants and their work in front of her. She responded with "f—- you very much!" According to Liz, Jean said there was a pause, and the room was so quiet that "you could have heard a gnat fart." Then, the executive turned to Jean and started laughing. This gave everyone else permission to laugh too.

"Jean got away with speaking truth to power because she appeared harmless. She wasn't in a power suit and didn't look intimidating. But, executives learned not to push her. I, in turn, learned that clients can take it. You don't have to treat them with kid gloves," Liz commented.

Jean was a master at speaking her truth with a light touch. As a lifelong learner, she had studied the court jester and commedia dell'arte traditions. She applied this to being playful when confronting executives. And, Jean modeled this well for Liz, whose own natural humor flourished under her mentor's guidance. "She taught me to be playful yet effective in the corporate world. I'm also a truth teller. I learned how to speak truth without blowing people out of the water," Liz remarked.

An opportunity for Liz to speak truth to power came when she returned to the IT department after completing her internship. On her first day back, she learned she'd been promoted to a staff role reporting to a department director, but she hadn't yet met the director in person. That same day, Liz also learned about her first project from a coworker, who was leaving the department, not from her new boss. Her colleague explained that the director wanted her to develop a partnership training program between IT and Kaiser doctors based on a Boston University model. Liz was baffled and annoyed that her director had communicated her new assignment through a peer.

When meeting her director in person for the first time, Liz bluntly asked, "Is this initiative just for show, or will we be living what we're teaching?" Her director replied that they'd definitely be living it. So, Liz stated, "Then we have a problem in the way the assignment was communicated to me. It doesn't reflect the partnership values I see in the model. If we don't talk about what's most important to you, I don't know how I can meet your objectives for this training." Her director responded, "You're absolutely right. I won't do that to you again. Thanks for speaking up." They set up a meeting and discussed the initiative. Liz credited Jean for modeling authentic behavior.

Learning on a Lot of Levels

After Liz returned to IT, her director agreed to contract her out part-time to co-lead training classes with Jean for the OD group because Liz's services were in high demand. Through her ongoing collaboration with Jean, Liz honed her training skills. Jean modeled effective training principles — never talk more than 12 minutes at a time, stick to the content, and engage learners through increasingly advanced exercises and practice activities supported by coaching. Liz called this "getting out of the way and getting learners talking and doing things." These principles had been ingrained in Jean through her UMass adult education program.

Beyond technical skills, Liz also learned from Jean how to show up in the corporate world. She reminisced, "It was amazing to discover that I could be fully myself, make a contribution, be effective and valuable, not get fired, and enjoy myself. This meant a lot because as a musician and music therapist, making the transition to corporate life was confusing. I was used to feeling pure bliss when performing with other musicians. I literally had to learn how to socialize and still be myself." She recalled a time when she had to ask friends why people go out for social dinners because she had never done that as an introverted musician.

Part of Liz's corporate learning was leveraging Kaiser's

resources for her professional development. She recalled, "Jean taught me to go outside OD to learn more broadly. She turned me on to new skills that would never have occurred to me as relevant to OD. For example, together we attended an Omega Institute week-long clowning course, and she showed me how to connect the dots so Kaiser would enthusiastically foot the bill." The purpose of studying clowning was to learn about handling authority figures with a light touch and to be comfortable with mistakes.

Liz shared an experience when taking the course that taught her about keeping mishaps in perspective. Every morning on their way to class, she and Jean would stop at a local grocery store to pick up sandwiches and drinks. It was rainy and windy, so Liz purchased lunch while Jean brought the car around to pick her up. Liz spotted Jean waving to her. At that moment, Liz dropped the bag of food. She described what happened next.

"Everything splashed out, including cans of drinks. It was just like the dropping exercise from our clown class where we attempt to pick up several things, but never succeed. The cans were rolling away from me in the wind. My hand disability meant I dropped things constantly, which I found embarrassing, so I struggled to get everything back into the bag. I looked up at Jean apologetically. She was leaning on the car doubled over laughing. Then, I started laughing so hard that I literally fell down on the wet pavement. The other shoppers were stepping over me. Jean staggered over to help me. We were weeping with laughter and soaking wet by the time we got everything in the car. That was the last time dropping something embarrassed me. Instead, it became a game, something I could play with to crack myself up."

Precious lessons from Jean continued after they both left Kaiser. Jean retired from the organization in 1995 and started her own OD consulting firm. Liz was laid off in 1996 and joined Jean as a junior partner. They served primarily San Francisco Bay Area clients, but also traveled to the East Coast and Ireland for consulting gigs.

"I learned from Jean how to get consulting work by net-working. She was so well connected that she would literally walk into the Kaiser credit union and come back with work. She also had colleagues who referred work to us. This taught me the necessity of networking. As a musician, that wasn't something I ever had to work at," Liz recalled.

Taking on new challenges was a huge part of Liz's growth as the junior partner. Jean taught a consulting skills class with a team of UMass alumni colleagues that she and her colleagues had co-developed. Over time, Jean foresaw the need to train new instructors to keep the class alive. So, she brought Liz along to observe a class and gave her the teacher's guide. Jean's colleagues started objecting to this, but Liz was already teaching. "Jean was fearless about what she wanted. What started out as a five-day class went to three days, and she really wanted a co-trainer. As far as I know, I ended up being the only person still teaching the course outside academia. I finally wrote my own version this year," Liz explained.

A good mentor knows when to push her mentee to do more, and Jean did that from the beginning. According to Liz, "Jean challenged me by opening doors and saying 'walk through.' Then she gave me feedback on what went well and what I needed to improve. Sometimes it wasn't much fun to listen, but it made a difference. I was very lucky."

Building on Jean's Legacy

Liz described her evolution in the OD firm with Jean. "I gradually moved from junior partner to full-fledged business partner. Jean started asking me to do things she no longer wanted to do. She was enjoying consulting less and less and eventually returned to part-time teaching in the Organizational Studies doctoral program at the California School of Professional Psychology (CSPP) in Alameda." So, Liz took over and ran the firm without Jean starting in 1998. She was finding her own voice.

After Alliant University bought CSPP, Jean was scheduled to teach a weekend consulting skills class at the Fresno campus. She was diagnosed with ovarian cancer on a Wednesday, went into surgery the next day, and the class was slated to start that Friday evening. Naturally, she asked Liz to cover for her. What was supposed to be a temporary project turned into a 14-year gig for Liz that extended well after Jean's death.

Over the years, Liz has rebranded her collaboration-focused, consulting firm with her own imprint, renaming it, and changing her offerings to keep up with her clients' interests and what excites her. She develops her own materials now, but still does a lot of meeting facilitation. Liz quipped, "I really thought I could change the meeting culture in organizations, which was just terrible when I started. And I think I have. Meetings are *much* worse now than they used to be. Through online technology, now we can bore hundreds of people at once. They can be even more passive and disengaged!"

Liz has become a highly respected consultant, facilitator,

and trainer in the Bay Area. And, she is exploring fascinating, new horizons that are bringing her full circle to her early, musician-in-flow experience. She has been trained in the Masterson Method of bodywork on horses. Liz is experimenting with applying this method to help dementia patients and their caregivers communicate more effectively.

She expressed her passion for this new frontier. "The body work I'm doing with horses comes closer to the way it feels to play music with others – the flow, the magic, the way it becomes something else that is such a delight. With the horses, it's a kind of dance, and being in rhythm is essential. As I work on them, they work on me. In corporate work, people resist and mistrust that flow." She's finding her voice in a new way.

Practicing Gratitude

Liz gives enormous credit to Jean for the impact on her life. "I'm grateful for what I learned from Jean. It took years off my learning curve. I went in a direction that was truer to myself because of her. It would have taken a lot longer to figure out on my own. She helped me through a very difficult, transitional time and got me on the right path. Then, she shoved me out of the nest when our paths started to diverge."

Liz knows her path would have been different without Jean's generosity and guidance. She observed, "Jean used gratitude as a practice long before positive psychology came along. I am so grateful to have had her as a mentor."

CHAPTER 12

TURNING RIGHT INSTEAD OF LEFT

*"I thank God for my destiny that put me in this position
with help from my parents, brother, and friends. I
cannot say that I've done this all by myself."*

✋

ORN IN 1965, Issa Abudakar encountered significant challenges as a boy. His father, Hassan, and mother, Aisha, were raising their growing family in a Palestinian immigrant camp in Zarka, Jordan. Issa recalled, "Our town had lots of camps with temporary housing the government had built for Palestinians from Israel. Many thousands of immigrants had migrated during the 1948 Palestine War and the Six Day War in 1967. The government didn't want people to build permanent homes because the immigration was expected to be temporary."

But, most immigrants never returned to their home country. So, Issa, his four brothers, five sisters, and parents eventually moved into a two-bedroom house with a metal roof. "I am the sixth child and was the only male who stuck around at a young age. My older brothers moved out of the house when they turned 17. And, I was in charge because my father was gone a lot," Issa explained.

Jobs in Jordan were scarce, so Hassan traveled to Saudi Arabia and other neighboring countries 11 months of the year to work as a mechanic and bus driver. He sent money home to Aisha so she could feed and clothe the family. Issa remembered how Hassan would supplement the family income with his electronic skills. "I used to watch my dad fix radios and televisions when he got home late at night. He could take them apart and put them back together by getting parts from other radios and televisions. And, he would get higher frequencies so we could listen to FM." Hassan was especially interested in reaching America to listen to English.

Aisha's superpowers were maximizing resources and bargaining. With an allowance from Hassan, she would trek to the local markets and buy shirts and pants for the kids. Issa recalled that "she would buy the next larger size or two because we grew so fast, and she wanted to make sure the clothes would last at least a year or so." If the salesperson was asking the equivalent of $30, she would typically buy the item for less than a quarter of that. Issa didn't know it at the time, but he was learning valuable negotiating skills that would serve him well in his future career.

Dreaming About His Own Business

"My parents did a wonderful job raising 10 kids on their income," Issa observed. And, their financial struggles made a deep impression on him. "My brother, Mohammed, who is 10 years older than me, left Jordan for Portland, Oregon, at age 20. When I was 12, I decided that one day I would follow in his footsteps and go to business school. And, I wanted to open my own business from the time I was a kid," he reminisced.

Issa seized his first entrepreneurial opportunity at age 14. His high school had no cafeteria, so many of the students ate homemade sandwiches during a half-hour recess. But, the more adventurous ones jumped over a wall and bought restaurant sandwiches across the road.

He approached the school principal with an idea. Issa explained, "I asked him for the use of an empty classroom and storage area and told him that I would negotiate with a restaurant if I could leave class 15 minutes early. My plan was to buy sandwiches and set up a school cafeteria. The principal asked how I'd pay for the food, and I said that I'd collect money from the students. I was prepared to pay one third less than what the restaurant owner was charging to buy 50 sandwiches at a time. I also told him that I'd share any profits with other student co-investors at the end of the year."

The principal liked Issa's plan, so his high school got its first cafeteria. The space where he set up the cafeteria had two windows overlooking the playground. This allowed students to pay for their orders outside one window and pick up their orders outside the other window during the recess. At the end of the year, Issa shared a 25 percent profit after expenses with his fellow student co-investors. Then, other schools in the area copied Issa's idea and started their own cafeterias.

He credited his mother, an early mentor, for his first entrepreneurial success because Aisha had modeled essential bargaining skills.

Looking Ahead to College

Issa's parents instilled in their kids the importance of getting a good education because it had been beyond their own reach. He described the challenges he faced in achieving that goal. "If you were Palestinian, you had to be in the top 10 percent of high school graduates to get into the university you wanted. Jordanian nationals were given preference over Palestinians. So, I realized that I'd either have to leave Jordan for a better opportunity or try my best to get good grades and be accepted into a top Jordanian university. My father pushed me to use my brain, do my homework, and go to a good school. He used to brag to our relatives when his kids did well in school."

But, Issa's grade point average (GPA) when he finished high school was only 2.4. He attributed this to having "too much on my plate during those years." As the oldest male still living at home, his high school study time was severely limited because Issa had to go with Aisha to buy and carry food home every day due to lack of refrigeration. Then, he would return to the market before closing and bring home food scraps for the family's sheep, rabbits, and chickens. But, by the time Issa graduated, his youngest brother was old enough to go to the market with Aisha. This meant that Issa could focus on higher education.

Absorbing Life Lessons for the Future

During his formative years, Issa absorbed countless, valuable lessons from his other early mentor, Hassan, who shaped his son's character and laid the foundation for Issa's future success.

He paid tribute to Hassan's wisdom and depth, whose

lessons were varied and rich. "My father was quiet and soft spoken, and he listened more than he talked. He used to say that God created us with two ears and one mouth so that we listen more than we talk. He impressed upon me that people judge us by how we act and talk, so it's important to be patient and not respond before thinking." Honesty with self and others was another repeated message.

And, Hassan taught Issa to have faith in others and give people the benefit of the doubt. "He trusted and respected others unless they gave him a reason not to. I still do that myself," Issa commented.

Beyond valuable interpersonal skills, Issa received guidance that would serve him well in completing his education and ultimately becoming an entrepreneur. He recalled how he learned from his father "to not give up, but to keep working hard because you will eventually be rewarded." And, when the rewards came, both Hassan and Aisha emphasized the importance of knowing how to spend and invest money.

Hassan's guidance was grounded in a positive mindset. Issa recalled, "My father used to say that every problem has a solution, and for every uphill climb, there is a downhill side. He believed that after life brings sorrow, there will come an easier time. This has definitely proved to be true many times in my life."

Planning His Migration to America

Fortified by Hassan's precious lessons, Issa set out to apply for a student visa to attend college in the U.S. After graduating from high school, he and three friends drew straws to see who would apply to the U.S. and who would target England as the destination. Issa explained what happened. "Two of the friends got U.S. student visas because they had 3.8 and 3.7 GPAs, and their families had more money than mine, so they could support themselves as students. I was refused a visa because my grades weren't high enough, and I didn't have much money to support myself."

He continued, "I didn't tell them at the embassy that I had a brother in Portland, where I'd be able to live as a student. I didn't want them to think I intended to stay in the U.S. after finishing college. I was planning a business major, which would take four years. They wanted to hear that I would return to Jordan."

Issa ended up applying 17 times for the U.S. student visa, which took 18 months. To improve his grades and chances of getting the visa, he enrolled in the Intermediate International College in Amman, Jordan, and studied accounting for two years.

Valentine's Day 1984 was auspicious. Issa got an interview with a counselor at the embassy, and the counselor asked if he spoke English. Issa recalled, "I don't know why I said 'yes.' The counselor started speaking with me in English, and I kept asking him to repeat himself. After a few minutes, he commented that he didn't think I spoke any English and brought an interpreter into the room. They asked me why I had applied 17 times, and I said that I wanted to go to the U.S. since I was a little kid. I tried to reassure them that I would return to Jordan, but they thought I'd stay in America because I would meet a woman. They asked me to promise to return to Jordan, and I promised. In my mind, I was thinking I'd go back to visit, but not to stay."

The counselor liked Issa's determination, so despite

expressing reservations, he granted the visa. "He told me he thought I would do very well in America. So, I moved to Portland when I was 19 and lived with my brother, Mohammed. My other two high school friends who had come before me were also living there," Issa reminisced.

Adapting to a New Life

Mohammed provided much more than a roof over Issa's head. He became his younger brother's mentor in America and had already established himself as a computer programmer for the City of Portland when Issa moved in with him. It would become a 30-year career by the time Mohammed retired.

Issa described his older brother as "mellow, funny, very smart, private, and disliking confrontations with loud people." A humble man devoted to helping people, Mohammed worked hard to guide Issa literally in the right direction.

"When I first came to the U.S., Mohammed told me there were two ways I could go. He compared it to driving on the freeway. After exiting, you can either turn right or left. If I turned right, I'd go to school, get my degree, and work hard toward my future. He also said there's a lot of temptation in America and that, if I turned left, I'd get into drugs and meet bad people. It was my choice to make every morning which way I would turn," Issa recalled.

Choosing to turn right, Issa enrolled in Portland Community College and began his business studies. Mohammed drove him to and from school each day. The older brother shared a lot of practical advice about surviving and thriving in America. Issa learned the basics from Mohammed, like the importance of meeting people on time, organizing his life, and establishing credit. "In Jordan, people think nothing of being an hour or two late. And, credit doesn't exist there. Everything is done with cash. He also advised me to make my payments on time because nothing is free," Issa explained. Perhaps most important of all, Mohammed urged Issa to always be honest with himself and truthful in his business dealings.

Working While Attending School

To pay for school, Issa got a job as a waiter and busboy at the Greenwood Inn in Portland. He reminisced about this job and his thoughts for the future. "I was one of the best waiters and was making $50 to $60 a day in cash. I told Mohammed that I didn't want to continue on to Portland State University (PSU), and instead wanted to start a business because I was making good money. I told him that if I graduated and worked as an accountant, I wouldn't make $50 to $60 a day."

Mohammed strongly encouraged Issa to stick to his plan and enroll in PSU. "He asked me what I wanted my future to be and reminded me that I came here to get an education and better my life. And, he repeated the choice that I must make when I get up every morning," Issa recalled.

So, Issa made another right turn and enrolled in PSU. He graduated with a Bachelor of Arts in business administration in 1991 with a 3.4 GPA.

Becoming an Entrepreneur

Issa finally got his first opportunity for a business after graduation. With capital that Mohammed invested, they opened a Plaid Pantry convenience store in Southeast Portland, the Burnside Market and Deli, in 1991. They sold the store two years later for a small profit.

Their next venture was a gas station that they purchased in 1995 in Vancouver, Washington. But, the commute north from Portland proved to be impractical. So, Issa and Mohammed sold that business a few months later.

Before opening these businesses, Issa benefited once again from Mohammed's wise guidance. The older brother prepared him for what to expect if he wanted to succeed as an entrepreneur. Issa recalled, "He told me that I would have to be willing to risk losing my entire capital investment, I would work very long hours, and I would have a lower quality of life until the business was established." Mohammed also emphasized the high stress, big responsibility, and risk of discouragement that go along with being an entrepreneur.

The underlying theme of Mohammed's advice was the necessity of a strong work ethic to achieve success. "America was still new to me, and while I had wanted to go to school and work, I also wanted to go out with my friends, have fun, and waste valuable time. My weakness was not keeping track of time. Mohammed sat me down and told me I needed to gain control of my time if I wanted to reach my full potential, be recognized for my efforts, and make a difference in what I accomplished. So, I made the businesses we invested in together my full focus," Issa explained.

Learning the Hospitality Industry

Issa took a 10-year hiatus from owning a business and learned the hospitality industry as an employee. Drawing on his skills as a waiter and busboy, he joined a Portland Hilton Hotel in 1995 and "gained a lot of experience there." Starting as a banquet captain, he became an assistant manager, and ultimately advanced to food and beverage director.

Taking Entrepreneurship to a New Level

But, by 2005, Issa was more than ready for a new entrepreneurial endeavor. He explained, "I found that the Peachtree Restaurant and Pie House in Vancouver was for sale. They were asking close to $1 million just for the business. I tried to get Mohammed to be my partner, but he didn't want to invest that much money in a restaurant. I believed in the Peachtree and knew that I could make money out of it. So, because of my brother's advice about the importance of building credit, I went to a bank and got a loan. I mortgaged my house for a 20 percent down payment. And, I drew upon my mom's negotiating techniques in the Jordanian markets to get the best deals from vendors. All the hard work and the investment paid off. I made a good income for myself and my family until I sold the restaurant in 2015."

Issa also purchased the Oak Tree Restaurant in Woodland, Washington, in 2008, and sold it in 2011. Both of these restaurants featured typical American food for breakfast, lunch, and dinner.

But, Issa would share the cuisine of his culture through his next business venture. During the 10 years he owned the Peachtree, he routinely cooked traditional Jordanian food in the evenings for his wife and kids, and he commented that they "just loved the food." Issa had learned the recipes from Aisha, who he described as "a very good cook."

Then, one day in 2014, Issa and his wife were in the parking lot of an east Vancouver commercial area and spotted a "for lease" sign on a large, vacant retail space. He recalled, "My wife said, 'You're a very good cook. Why don't you open a Middle Eastern restaurant?' So, I thought about it for a day or two, then got ahold of the owner and signed a lease. With my mom's help, we created the menu. We decided to call it 'Petra House' because we wanted something that had name recognition and would be easy for Americans to remember. Petra is a well-known, historical city in Jordan, and we were going to serve Jordanian food."

Serving Savory Food in an Exotic Ambience and Earning Rave Reviews

Petra House has become a thriving restaurant and beloved community gathering place. There's a reason it has earned 756 Google reviews averaging 4.5 as of this writing.

Inspired by his home country, Issa has created an exotic ambience of rich, colorful fabrics; private booths with floor seating; camel figures, ornate objects, and other Middle Eastern art. Jordanian music wafts through the sound system. Gracious servers in traditional robes greet patrons and drip warm rose water from pewter vessels over their hands before taking food orders. They pour mint tea from decorative pots into dainty cups and serve Turkish coffee spiced with cardamom in classic ibrik pots.[17]

The menu features a long list of Aisha's special dishes. Among the many wonderful choices are appetizers of hummus and baba ghanoush (smoked eggplant with green peppers, tomatoes, garlic, and lemon juice in tahini sauce garnished with black olives). Lamb shank and mujaddara (a lentil and rice casserole) are some of the most popular, traditional dishes. A "favorites" section offers shawarma (marinated chicken, beef, and lamb), gyros, and a variety of kababs. And, to satisfy their sweet tooth, patrons are tempted by baklava and other intriguing desserts.

Members of Issa's family prepare the food. And, until she died in March 2019, Aisha was frequently by Issa's side at the restaurant, drawing quiet satisfaction from her son's successful creation. He described her reaction to Petra House. "My mother loved the way we did the décor. She felt it resembled Jordan and Palestine. She also loved how we brought the culture to American people and introduced her recipes."

So, Petra House has meant much more to Issa than simply another successful business venture. It has been his way of connecting Jordan and America. And, to preserve his connection with Jordan, he traveled back to his home country four times between 1994 and 2019.

---

17 During the COVID-19 pandemic, Issa complied with the Washington State order that limited service to takeout and delivery for several months.

Giving Back

Issa is committed to giving back and sharing his success. He has become the business mind in the family and now offers advice to Mohammed on purchases and investments. He has also contributed generously to his community over many years. This generosity has taken a variety of forms – providing free meals after high school games, donating 10 percent of what parents spend at his restaurants for sports programs, and bringing Jordanian food to school cultural events. Issa has been equally generous with his time through the Vancouver Chamber of Commerce and his mosque. He cited an example. "When I was a vice president and board member of our mosque, we invited the local Christian and Jewish communities to come meet with us once a year and learn about our religion of peace."

Planning for the Future

In addition to managing Petra House and giving back to his community, Issa is looking ahead four years to when his youngest child will graduate from college. He plans to retire at that point to "spend more time with my family, travel the world, and enjoy myself before I get too old to travel" – a wonderful reward for a lifetime of hard work.

Cherishing His Mentors

Issa reflected on his success and gave enormous credit to others. "I thank God for my destiny that put me in this position with help from my parents, brother, and friends. I cannot say that I've done this all by myself."

He "cherished every minute" he spent with Hassan during his father's lifetime, and Mohammed remains very special to Issa. He commented, "I try to take what I learned from them and share it with my kids. When my father passed away 10 years ago, it changed my life completely. I became a better person. He taught me that whatever you plant, that's what you'll harvest. You take your good deeds and good reputation with you. A lot of people back home remember my father's legacy – what a good and honest person he was. And, I've had the best relationship with Mohammed that a brother could have. We're very close."

Issa concluded, "Both my father and Mohammed told me they were proud of what I have accomplished, and they talked about my success back home. I'm very happy that I made them proud and that their time mentoring me was well spent."

Chapter 13

Connecting the Dots Across the Stories

"When the student is ready, the teacher will appear."

— Origin uncertain
(sometimes attributed to the Theosophical Society)[18]

✧

W HEN I BEGAN interviewing mentees to capture their stories, I had no idea what I would learn. I only knew the truth of my own mentoring experience. I approached the interviews with an open mind. So, it was enlightening to discover common themes emerging across the stories – even after the first few interviews. The more people I interviewed, the more their experiences revealed the themes.

As stated in chapter 2, the seven themes capture three aspects of the mentoring process:

---

18   Fake Buddha Quotes. Accessed April 1, 2020. https://fakebuddhaquotes.com/when-the-student-is-ready-the-teacher-will-appear/.

Connecting with the Mentor

> Being ready at the right time to receive a mentor
> Enjoying shared passion and personal chemistry

Learning from the Mentor

> Learning from role models – professionally and personally
> Feeling safe to show vulnerability
> Accepting challenges to learn what we didn't know we needed

Evolving into Independence from the Mentor

> Experiencing the relationship evolve organically
> Leaving the nest

The seven themes are described below along with representative examples from the stories.

Being Ready at the Right Time to Receive a Mentor

There is no "readiness" switch that we can turn on to bring a mentor into our life. However, readiness is a mindset that we can cultivate to help create the conditions for mentors to appear. I cover this in chapter 14 where I share the "readiness" advice of the mentees.

Mentors emerge through an organic process, as expressed in the quote above, "When the student is ready, the teacher will appear." Chuck Bender provided a powerful example, describing the conditions that led to meeting Donald Sandner. "I don't know how I got invited to the 'Friends of Jung' dinner with Don Sandner. Someone in the organization must have thought that would be an interesting relationship for me. There are mysterious forces helping us get what we need."

And, the element of surprise is frequently at play. Our mentors appear when we're ready and often when we don't expect them.

My own readiness was triggered by answering an employment ad in the *Westport News*. This led to an interview with the man whose influence would shape my professional and personal life well beyond the years that we worked together.

Therese Brooks just wanted to take a few classes for intellectual stimulation. Her childcare schedule drove her to sign up for Jeannie Raffa's dream class – a serendipity that made all the difference in Therese's life.

Kevin Jordan's compliance career at Kaiser Permanente had run its course. He was looking for his next challenge, so he applied for a new position in a different part of the organization. Little did he know at the time that his next manager, Peter Richter, would open career doors that Kevin couldn't imagine at the time.

Donna Sinclair loved learning. So, as a single mother of three young children, she enrolled in Washington State University Vancouver to pursue her bachelor's degree. She had no idea that two of her professors would become mentors and mold her public history career.

A friend advised Russell Delman to study with Moshe Feldenkrais if he ever had the opportunity. Then, a flier advertising Moshe's first North American training program for $5,000 arrived in Russell's mailbox. He had just inherited $5,000 from his mother. So, Russell attended the training program – a seminal early step in what ultimately led to his founding *The Embodied Life* international school of awareness.

Liz Williams was stymied over how to restart her career for the third time after severe back and hand injuries. In the last class before pausing her master's program, her teacher happened to mention a Kaiser Permanente internship. Liz took the tip seriously and pursued the internship. Had she not done that, she never would have met Jean Westcott, a mentor who set Liz on the path to becoming a respected consultant, facilitator, and trainer.

Enjoying Shared Passion and Personal Chemistry

> *Chuck Bender described the energy that fuels mentor-mentee relationships. "A deep recognition takes place between two people who share a passion for something. There's a two-way resonance"– like the "kinship" he felt with Don Sandner. Shared passion and personal chemistry go hand-in-hand.*

My shared passion with Fermo Gianesello was effective communication. With a love of writing that started as a child, I had launched my professional life as a journalist, then entered the corporate world as a newsletter writer. But, I was eager to broaden my business communication skills. I wanted to learn from Fermo more about marketing writing, visual communication, publication design, and print production. I also welcomed mastering presentation skills and product training programs. Our wonderful chemistry was a blend of his kind-hearted desire to take me under his wing and my youthful enthusiasm to learn.

Shortly before starting the APR 6 program under his dad's mentorship, Bennett Brandenburg discovered a new side of Barry – his deeply caring nature. Bennett witnessed his dad in his counselor role offering fatherly guidance to a troubled, at-risk client. It was a paradigm shift for Bennett, and it transformed his perspective on practicing law. He realized that his job was to be "a person first and a lawyer second." Their shared passion for serving people drew them closer and elevated their personal and professional relationship to new levels.

Rebecca Keith chose to receive her training from Ursula Thrush because of their shared passion for Montessori education and the strong connection that Rebecca immediately felt to Ursula. "She was so much more in tune with what mattered to me. Her enthusiasm, energy, dedication, love of what she did, and deep understanding of the Montessori philosophy really spoke to me," Rebecca recalled.

John Greene found Jean-Pierre Mentha to be "a kindred spirit" who shared John's minority perspective that universities primarily exist to teach students and that research is a secondary purpose. His mentor's naturally gregarious nature and ease with conversation enhanced their early bonding over common interests.

After attending an initial session of Jeannie Raffa's class on dreams, Therese Brooks was "blown away, awestruck." Jeannie awakened in Therese a passion for exploring the unconscious. They formed a strong, personal connection over many years, focusing on the work of Carl Jung and dream symbolism. And, she was initially drawn to her second mentor, Martha Blake, because of their shared interest in Jung and dreams.

Donna Sinclair had always loved history, so she was hooked in her first class with Bill Lang, experiencing him as "a brilliant, erudite lecturer" who introduced her "to different ways of thinking about the past." Donna had many epiphanies in Bill's classes and found that her mind "clicked with his." Years later, he told Donna that she was "the best student" he ever had. And, she initially connected with her other significant mentor, the prominent Native American historian, Jackie Peterson, because of her fierceness and intellect. Although Jackie was "tough" on her students, she took Donna under her wing because she recognized Donna's innate talent. Love of history attracted Donna to Bill and Jackie, and mutual respect fueled their long relationships.

Issa Abudakar shared with his mother, father, and older brother a passion for creatively using the resources at their disposal. Aisha stretched their limited money by buying the kids' clothing in sizes they could wear longer. Hassan supplemented their income by reusing old parts to repair and sell radios and televisions. Issa recognized that an empty classroom and storage area could be repurposed as a profitable cafeteria. And, Mohammed viewed time as a precious resource, so he instilled the importance of time management in Issa as a young entrepreneur. The chemistry that connected them was their common values – hard work, honesty, respect, trust, positivity, discipline, humility, and generosity.

Learning from Role Models – Professionally and Personally

The core of mentoring is serving as a role model. Mentees learn by listening to instructions, applying advice, practicing new skills, and completing assignments. But, the most powerful way we learn is by observing our mentors in action. They are exemplars of how to be in the world, often in a parental manner. And, their lessons are transferable to countless future situations. Our mentors develop us into whole human beings.

I have integrated a good deal into my life from all that Fermo taught me. As shared in my story, he modeled assertiveness, relating to colleagues on a human level, keeping commitments, integrity, strength, courage, resilience, positivity, joy, and adventure. His lessons have been a lighthouse at important points over the years.

The biggest lesson that Bennett Brandenburg learned from observing his father interact with clients was that "the law is about people, not strict guidelines." He didn't find this lesson in any law textbook. He witnessed the way Barry counseled a client in jail, hoping to steer her toward better life choices. It was a shift that put Bennett's entire law career in a more meaningful context. Barry also modeled mediating and collaborating with all parties involved in cases – rather than playing an adversarial role. And, despite the challenges of handling a demanding law practice, Bennett learned from his dad to keep his case hours under control, preserving precious family and personal time.

Ursula Thrush set a powerful example for Rebecca Keith – the necessity of taking risks to fulfill her calling. Ursula's passion for "education for peace and changing the world through education" drove her achievements. She sold her grandparents' beloved antique desk to raise the money for her training, moved with her son to America, learned English, founded a Montessori school and training center in San Francisco, and influenced the worldwide Montessori curriculum. This example inspired Rebecca's journey. She completed her Montessori training and formal education, founded her own school, took over Ursula's training center, launched the Montessori Phoenix Project, and has continued leading her school for over 40 years.

Jean-Pierre Mentha did much to shape John Greene's personality, which greatly enhanced his career success. His mentor taught John the value of acting out of empathy while setting aside personal emotions to deal effectively with university politics. John also gained humility; Jean-Pierre had "knocked a bit of youthful arrogance out of" him. Over the years, he refined his people skills, learning from Jean-Pierre how to be "a velvet hand in a velvet glove." Kindness, justice, intellectual rigor, and staying involved were other valuable lessons that John attributed to his mentor.

Peter Richter modeled well the attributes of exceptional leadership and professional growth for Kevin Jordan. The biggest lessons included collaboration, focus on the work, alignment of diverse interests, consensus-building, stretching beyond one's comfort zone, not taking things at face value, selfless teamwork, perpetual learning, trust, and honesty.

Russell Delman's learning from Moshe Feldenkrais was rich and deep. It began during the first professional training through experiential learning. Integration of physical, emotional, and mental patterns – the core of the Feldenkrais

Method – was an enormous, complex lesson in awareness. And, Moshe's rigorous practice of constantly questioning and looking at things from multiple perspectives deeply influenced Russell. This taught Russell to "always think freshly." Yet, despite his vast wisdom, Moshe also modeled authenticity. According to Russell, his mentor "was always just himself in the company of others and never put on airs."

Liz Williams had no idea that she could be her down-to-earth, genuine, fun self in the corporate world until she encountered Jean Westcott. Her mentor taught her the importance of speaking truth to power. And, Liz learned from Jean to sharpen her organizational skills in nontraditional ways, such as by taking a clowning course to help her handle authority figures with a light touch and be comfortable making mistakes. These lessons contributed enormously to building Liz's professional confidence and poise.

Issa Abudakar learned lifelong values from his mother, father, and older brother. He watched his mother diligently feed and clothe the family while his father traveled 11 months of the year to neighboring countries for work, which he supplemented by selling repaired televisions and radios. Hassan stressed with Issa the importance of being honest with oneself and others, respectful, and trusting of people. His father's positive belief that "every problem has a solution" guided Issa's life journey. And, Mohammed instilled in Issa the discipline to focus on his studies and grow his fledgling business rather than waste time. His brother delivered this message with humility and a generous spirit.

APPLYING MENTORS' LESSONS
WITH GREATER URGENCY

While writing this chapter, the COVID-19 outbreak was surging at a frightening rate in the United States. The pandemic was rapidly transforming everyone's life in ways that we couldn't have envisioned a few months earlier. So, I decided to reach out to the mentees I had interviewed. I was curious to know how their mentors' most significant life lessons sustained and helped them adapt during the outbreak – professionally and personally. Here's how several of them responded.

Bennett Brandenburg underscored his father's belief that the law is about people in the context of COVID-19. He commented, "Now I'm more focused on the personal stories of each client... and I'm able to appreciate their cause more than I used to... Perhaps there is a silver lining in all of this." He reiterated that the essence of his law practice is "developing healthy relationships with clients and connecting with their troubles empathically" – a perspective that his dad instilled when Bennett started the legal mentorship program.

Therese Brooks emphasized the increased importance of supporting her female clients "to cope with unexpected events and the demands of parenting."

Kevin Jordan shared a long list of lessons that Peter Richter had imparted over the years. Below were some of the most relevant lessons during the unfolding outbreak:

Health and family come first.

Take care of yourself. Have self-compassion.

We, the team, come before I and me. That's servant leadership.

Focus on what you can control, and let go of the rest.

Separate the signals from the noise. What's truly important and why?

Manage your energy, and your time will flow from that.

Be a force for good and positive change.

The perfect is the enemy of the good.

Walk your talk.

Know when to ask for help.

Seek to understand – before being understood.

Assume that others have the best of intentions until you learn otherwise.

Honor your values and what is right.

Treat others the way they want to be treated.

Russell Delman summarized the wisdom that he absorbed from Moshe Feldenkrais for troubled times. "Recognize that external conditions never determine our state. They influence, but do not cause our experience. Through awareness, we can stand in our freedom, which means the capacity to respond with a caring heart, even if it means, at first, caring for our own fears and confusion."

Issa Abudakar recalled his father's advice: "Always make sure to save money to survive for at least six months. Save your white penny for your dark days." So, when COVID-19 forced Washington restaurant closures – other than takeout and delivery – Issa had enough cash reserves to help weather the downturn in business. Like many other restaurants in the state, Issa switched to takeout and delivery. But, he also learned to create menu items that were faster to prepare, such as wraps and smaller portions that customers could purchase more often. And, he kept a database of customer contact information to send text notifications when Petra House would reopen for restaurant dining. Issa had learned well from his father that "every problem has a solution."

Feeling Safe to Show Vulnerability

We learn best when we feel safe enough to expose our vulnerabilities – weaknesses, self-doubts, lack of confidence, fears, and other uncontrolled emotions. Our mentors meet us where we are without judging us. Unless we have this safe learning environment, it is much harder to develop into the best version of ourselves.

When he began learning under his father's mentorship, Bennett Brandenburg was conflicted between being terrified that he'd never be a great lawyer like Barry and striving to do things his own way. But, as their mentor-mentee relationship developed, Bennett became comfortable sharing more and more of his vulnerable, emotional side with Barry, and his father reciprocated, which strengthened their bond.

Rebecca Keith felt safe enough with Ursula Thrush to assert that she wasn't confident to start an experimental kindergarten classroom after only two years of experience. She expressed her concern, and the strong-willed Ursula gave her an ultimatum to either do it or work elsewhere. Rebecca chose to find another teaching job. Although Ursula was initially angry, she came to accept Rebecca's decision. The relationship survived and thrived as they evolved into peers. Rebecca learned that she could be honest with her mentor, withstand her anger, witness Ursula come around, and grow in the process.

When John Greene discovered that funds he had counted on for a language center had been misappropriated, rather than containing his feelings, he revealed his outrage to his mentor. Jean-Pierre Mentha acknowledged John's feelings, then settled him down. He wisely advised John not to become a whistleblower, but instead to work through the proper channels to obtain funding. John found another funding source and avoided a nasty situation because he followed his mentor's advice.

Therese Brooks opened up to Jeannie Raffa at a deep, intimate level. She exposed her shadow to Jeannie – the unconscious, unknown aspects of her personality as revealed through her dreams. Together they examined Therese's family of origin issues and early childhood trauma, as manifested through co-dependency, alcoholism, unresolved grief, and loss. Jeannie embraced Therese's total self and guided her integration of masculine and feminine qualities.

Donna Sinclair didn't think she had any special talents when she first met Bill Lang. She was a struggling, single mother who simply wanted to complete her bachelor's degree and teach public school. He helped her strive for bigger goals and gave her "professional confidence in (her) talents." Jackie Peterson also appreciated Donna's raw talent and took her student under her wing.

Liz Williams felt extremely vulnerable when Jean Westcott introduced her to high-powered organization development colleagues. She recalled, "It was intimidating to be around people older and more accomplished. I was learning a new field, and my hands didn't work. I couldn't even shake hands when I met these influential people." But, Jean looked well beyond Liz's insecurities, encouraged her to learn from humorous mishaps, and guided her to grow into her full professional strength.

Issa Abudakar's biggest weakness as a young man, according to his older brother, Mohammed, was his tendency to lose track of time and not stay focused on work. Their trusting relationship and the respect that Issa had for Mohammed helped him absorb his brother's advice to buckle down. Issa learned to devote himself to the businesses he was building. Mohammed believed in Issa's potential and helped him overcome his flaws.

Accepting Challenges to Learn What We Didn't Know We Needed

Chuck Bender astutely observed that our mentors guide us to learn what we don't yet know we need along our professional development journey. And, they often deliver such learning by offering challenges for us to embrace.

As an introvert, I was happily cruising along in my publications editor role when Fermo Gianesello suggested that I tackle business presentations. I had never spoken in front of an audience, and he wanted me to address a sales organization of 100 older men at a national sales meeting. The notion terrified me at first. But, under his guidance, I diligently created and rehearsed the content before boarding a plane to Texas. Once at the hotel, I settled into the idea by getting to know many of the guys during the first two days of the meeting. That relaxed me enough to deliver my material with confidence on day three. Fermo saw my potential, and he pushed me to stretch my skills.

Rebecca Keith learned best from Ursula Thrush by being constantly thrown "into slightly bigger ponds all the time, like doing a presentation at a Montessori conference." It wasn't Ursula's style to coddle her mentee. Rebecca recalled, "She would tell me, 'get your act together and go do it.' She would challenge me to move from my comfort zone to something a little bit scarier." These experiences greatly accelerated Rebecca's growth and prepared her for future success.

Therese Brooks was savoring a wide range of classes at the Jung Center. She hadn't realized that she could advance her learning by teaching. But, Jeannie Raffa suggested that she run her own dream groups and lead a class. Therese embraced the challenge and created a class on the mother-daughter initiation into the conscious feminine. And, her second mentor, Martha Blake, posed the ultimate challenge – doing Jungian work professionally – when Therese still thought of her dream explorations as a hobby. Martha urged her to study at Pacifica Graduate Institute because the program would foster her continued process of individuation. Therese earned a Master of Arts in counseling psychology from Pacifica, became licensed, and launched her own private practice.

Before he even got a job offer from Peter Richter, Kevin Jordan declared his ambition for leadership development and career advancement. Peter responded by relentlessly presenting growth challenges. "Are you ready to be uncomfortable" was Peter's signal that he wanted Kevin to take on his next challenge. Kevin made director in four and a half years by consistently undertaking new development goals and stretch opportunities.

Russell Delman came of age during the San Francisco Human Potential Movement in the early 1970s. He had developed a world view that peace was good and war was evil. Then, Moshe Feldenkrais directly confronted his world view. Moshe taught him to think about war from multiple perspectives – certainly the evil it wrought, but also the advancements and evolution that resulted. Russell learned to embrace multiple points of view by actively questioning assumptions. Only then was holistic understanding possible, according to his wise mentor.

Experiencing the Relationship Evolve Organically

The relationships with our mentors evolve naturally over time. As we continue interacting with them in a variety of situations, we come to know our mentors in deeper, more intimate ways. We often become colleagues on an equal footing and even lifelong friends. We don't have to force the process. It happens organically.

Fermo Gianesello was my manager for five years. We had gotten to know one another so well that, by the time I left the organization for a new job, we had become friends. Over the remaining 15 years of our relationship, we occasionally socialized in person and stayed in touch by phone. He had been planning to attend my wedding. I was important to him. So, when Fermo suddenly died, a friend of his found my name in his address book and called me with the shocking news.

Bennett Brandenburg and his dad, Barry, had been "buddies my whole life," according to Bennett. But, as they took on the roles of mentor-mentee and Bennett struggled to find his footing in the law firm, they worked through their conflicts and eventually established new roles as equal partners. Today, they continue to seek each other's advice. A key aspect of this evolution was opening up to each other in more intimate ways.

Rebecca Keith eagerly welcomed the training she received

from Ursula Thrush. She took in the lessons, observed her mentor in action, and adapted the learning to fit her own style. Her decision to leave Ursula's school for another teaching job rather than start an experimental kindergarten was a turning point in their relationship. Later, Rebecca started helping Ursula in her San Francisco training center, which she took over many years later. And, they became lifelong friends, often socializing in Rebecca's home. They grew so close that Rebecca advocated for Ursula's care when her mentor was hospitalized and dying of cancer. In the end, the news of Ursula's death came to Rebecca intuitively. Their relationship continues inwardly to this day; Rebecca still dreams about her mentor.

Kevin Jordan collaborated with Peter Richter on an evolving set of development goals and stretch assignments. Along the way, he acquired a wide range of leadership and organization development skills from Peter. A lot of the learning took place over lunch and dinner conversations and during business trips. And, conversation would inevitably turn to personal matters, which fed a growing friendship. For a few years, Kevin and Peter were even peers on the same leadership team. Then, Peter continued mentoring Kevin in various roles until Kevin ultimately launched his own executive, leadership, and career transformation coaching practice. He commented, "Now our relationship is purely a friendship… Work was the base point of our relationship, but it hasn't defined us or been hugely instrumental in our lives for several years now."

Over time, Donna Sinclair's relationship with Bill Lang and Jackie Peterson evolved from student-professor to mentee-mentor to lifelong friends. In the classroom, Bill and

Jackie introduced the idea of history as a career. Then, they provided multiple, real world learning opportunities. Bill and Jackie connected her with respected professionals in their networks. And, along the way, they took a personal interest in her wellbeing as they began to socialize. Donna treasures her friendship with Bill and Jackie to this day.

When Russell Delman attended Moshe's first North American professional training program, he was initially intimidated by Moshe's abrupt communication style. But, he became increasingly more comfortable with Moshe over time. After Russell sustained a neck injury in a car accident, Moshe helped him dramatically relieve his pain. During that period, they started bonding in a more personal way. The next "big leap forward" in their relationship came when Russell applied Moshe's own techniques to help him recover from two strokes. When he learned that Moshe had suddenly died, Russell was deeply affected by the loss of the man who had become his teacher and friend over many years. According to Russell, "Moshe still lives in my heart and the background of my life."

Liz Williams first got to know Jean Westcott as a coach during her corporate training internship. Liz was drawn to Jean's unorthodox, authentic style of operating in the corporate world, and Jean appreciated Liz's raw talent. So, Jean took Liz under her wing and began opening doors by introducing her to high-powered colleagues. They gradually became peers when Liz started co-leading training classes with Jean. This evolved into a budding friendship developed over shared experiences. Their relationship advanced to a new level when Jean launched her own organization development consulting firm. Liz joined her – initially as a junior partner and later as a full partner. Then, Jean turned over the business to Liz to resume part-time teaching. They stayed connected until Jean's death, yet she is very much alive in Liz's grateful memory.

Leaving the Nest

When mentoring is successful, mentees eventually leave the nest. We integrate the precious lessons learned and make our own way in the world. This can take several forms – developing our personal style, paying it forward by mentoring others, and sometimes even swapping roles to mentor our mentors.

I left the nest when I took a new job with Citicorp. After five years with Dresser Industries, I was ready to move on and apply all that I had learned professionally and personally from Fermo Gianesello to the world of international, asset-based finance. He had prepared me well for a long, successful corporate career. Grounded in his lessons, I proceeded confidently to develop my voice and make a difference in multiple industries over many decades. And, a big part of this work was mentoring my younger colleagues, a role that Fermo had modeled so well.

John Greene's promotion to department chair and acceptance of other administrative roles were the visible manifestations of leaving Jean-Pierre Mentha's nest. The process of coming into his own had gradually unfolded as John learned from his mentor how to successfully navigate the university system. And, Jean-Pierre respected and leveraged the institutional influence that John wielded in his senior roles. Mentor and mentee had become equals in collaboration.

Furthermore, inspired by his own mentoring experience, John initiated a departmental mentoring program that was still active when he retired.

Leaving the first nest for Therese Brooks took place when she moved from Florida to Washington. Jeannie Raffa had influenced Therese's inner life so deeply that she sought a dream group after settling into her new home. Jeannie had firmly laid the groundwork for Therese to continue exploring her unconscious through her dreams and to undertake Jungian analysis with Martha Blake, her second mentor. Then, Therese left another nest when she embraced Martha's advice and transitioned Jungian psychology from hobby to profession. Today she mentors many of her own clients – women undergoing life transitions.

Moshe Feldenkrais prepared Russell Delman to leave the nest by urging him to develop his own handwriting. Moshe wanted Russell to "first learn well, then experience the freedom to improvise – be both diligent in your study and free in your thinking." Russell had numerous opportunities to do so. He gave back to Moshe by applying Feldenkrais techniques in his own way to help his mentor recover from two strokes. Russell has led many training classes in his personal style, mentoring numerous students. And, he has most especially developed his unique handwriting by creating and leading *The Embodied Life* school of awareness, which integrates Feldenkrais movement lessons with meditation and guided inquiry. As Moshe did with him, Russell helps his students discover their own handwriting.

Liz Williams began test flights out of Jean Westcott's nest by taking on greater responsibility and eventually became a full-fledged business partner in their consulting practice. For example, Jean brought Liz into her consulting skills faculty team of senior colleagues. Later, as new opportunities caught Jean's interest, she transitioned more and more of her role to Liz. When Liz eventually took over and ran the practice, she rebranded the business in her own style.

Issa Abudakar left his parents' nest – literally and figuratively – when he moved to the U.S. to complete his education and launch his first business. He carried with him years of valuable lessons for work and life. Upon arriving in the U.S., he landed in a new nest – his older brother's home in Portland, Oregon. Mohammed provided shelter along with a good deal of wise counsel. And, they became partners in a few early business ventures. Issa fully emerged from Mohammed's nest as he gained the confidence to proceed on his own. His first independent venture was purchasing the Peachtree Restaurant and Pie House, followed by the Oak Tree Restaurant. Then, he built his ultimate creation from scratch – Petra House. Issa has become the business mind of the family and now advises Mohammed on money matters.

CHAPTER 14

CULTIVATING A READINESS MINDSET AND NURTURING THE RELATIONSHIP

"All things are ready, if our mind be so."

– William Shakespeare, Henry V[19]

⚛

T HE STORIES IN this book demonstrate how mentors appear organically when mentees are ready to receive them. The process is much more art than science. As stated in chapter 13, *readiness is a mindset that we can cultivate to help create the conditions for mentors to appear.* And, beyond mindset, mentor-mentee relationships flourish if they are properly nurtured.

When interviewing the mentees, I asked them what advice they had to share on cultivating a readiness mindset and nurturing the mentoring relationship. This chapter captures their responses – and my own thoughts.

---

19 "Readiness Quotes," Good Reads. Accessed April 21, 2020. https://www.goodreads.com/quotes/tag/readiness.

Cultivating a Readiness Mindset

Cultivating a readiness mindset means being committed to exploration, curiosity, authentic relating, professional and personal development – as expressed below in a variety of ways.

Pursue Your Interests

Liz Williams recommended exploring your interests to discover a meaningful career. "Be aspirational. Be more than your resume. Have an aim that's about more than mere survival. A mentor has to see something in you that they want to support," she observed.

Seek a Life Role Model

For Bennett Brandenburg, it's essential to seek a person "who embodies what you want to do in your life and who challenges you." He added, "Be ready for a mentor to kick your butt, ask you to do things, examine yourself, go to dark places, and force you to realize that you haven't figured it all out."

"Ask yourself where and what you want to be. If you want to be successful, find someone who is successful. Gender and age don't matter," Issa Abudakar commented.

Identify Personal Qualities

Donna Sinclair suggested keeping your eyes open for someone with the qualities that you want to develop in yourself. She advised, "Pay attention to how they interact with others and how they're perceived. What's their reputation? Who are they as professionals? Do they care about others?"

In a similar vein, John Greene advised looking for someone "you respect and admire as a person, not just a colleague."

Commit to Authenticity

Rebecca Keith focused on the importance of looking for "someone with whom you have chemistry and are able to feel safe and be honest." She added, "Don't look for prestige or credentials."

Likewise, Kevin Jordan emphasized really getting to know another person and letting the mentoring process evolve organically. He also underscored developing a relationship with someone you can trust.

Strive to Expand Your Capacity

Therese Brooks advised allowing events to unfold naturally and being curious about them. She commented, "If you catch yourself saying 'I never thought of it that way,' it's a good sign that you may have found your mentor. Look for someone who expands your capacity for understanding, relating to, and seeing yourself."

Aim to Keep Company with Those Who Say "Look!"

The line from Mary Oliver's poem, *Mysteries, Yes*, "Let me keep company always with those who say 'Look!' and laugh in astonishment, and bow their heads," resonates deeply with Russell Delman. He characterized this sense of wonder as an essential quality to identify in a mentor.

Complete the Parenting Experience

Finally, I offer my own advice. For those of us who had an incomplete parenting experience, I recommend being open to someone who really sees us and can provide the guidance and role modeling that we missed growing up. Fermo Gianesello became a father figure to me by imparting life lessons and wisdom, which went way beyond career development.

Nurturing the Relationship

Successful mentoring requires give and take between mentor and mentee. That said, much of the responsibility falls on the shoulders of the mentee to nurture the relationship.

Drive the Process

Kevin emphasized the importance of committing to the relationship, respecting the mentor's time, proactively driving the process, and asking specific questions to stimulate focused, productive conversations.

Donna commented, "You must make a conscious choice to develop a relationship with a mentor. Organize the meetings. Come prepared. Ask thoughtful questions, and don't take advantage of their time."

According to Therese, a successful mentoring relationship requires that the mentee is intentionally dedicated to the Jungian individuation process (becoming one's whole self, as defined in chapter 7) and makes sufficient time to do the work.

Listen with Intention

"Practice the art of listening. It's not waiting to talk. When you ask a mentor what you should do, it's not asking to be told what you want to hear. Trust your mentor's wisdom and chew on the advice," Bennett recommended.

Issa's version of this was to "take every piece of advice because it will pay off – if not now, then in the future." He elaborated, "Be open-minded to your mentor's opinion, even if it's hard to hear. And, ask for help when you need it."

Observe Behavior

"By all means, ask for advice, but also observe your mentor's behavior," John noted. He added that it's equally important to show your vulnerability, express your doubts, and discuss your feelings.

I learned the most from Fermo by watching him in action. I consciously assessed what worked so well for him that I could adapt to my own style. Even to this day, I occasionally ask myself, "What would Fermo do in this situation?"

Maintain the Right Balance

To Russell, a healthy mentoring relationship requires maintaining a balance between being empowered and challenged. He advised actively paying attention to how a mentor makes you feel. "If they make you feel less than, walk away. Especially if they act like their way is the only way, walk away. On the other hand, if they are unwilling to challenge you, walk away," Russell commented.

Provide Something in Return

"Mentoring is a mutually beneficial relationship, so you must have something to offer your mentor by being interesting, three dimensional. It's much bigger than you simply needing help or throwing yourself at people," Liz noted.

Rebecca agreed that mentoring is "a two-way street, and the mentee must provide a valuable experience for the mentor to learn as well. Often we don't know what we don't know until we try to teach someone else."

Finally, Bennett, Kevin, and Issa commented that reversing roles has deepened their relationships. Bennett's dad, Barry, now sometimes requests his son's advice. As friends, Kevin and Peter occasionally mentor each other. And, at this stage in his life, Issa shares financial advice with his brother, Mohammed.

Making the Mentoring Difference

Mentoring starts with another person recognizing our raw talent. Then, our mentors guide and inspire us to develop this talent and achieve our full potential. We are not the same as when we first met them. We are transformed. They have shaped us, and we are now more self-actualized – professionally and personally. They have made the mentoring difference.

So, go forth and embrace mentoring. May it make all the difference for you and those you mentor.

CONNECTING IN THE COVID-19 WORLD AND BEYOND

The observations from mentees in this chapter touch on important aspects of connecting and relating. And, human beings have always relied heavily on face-to-face interactions to make this happen. Then, COVID-19 struck, disrupting nearly every aspect of our lives, including forcing us to interact with one another differently. So, what does this mean for mentoring in a world where health experts say we're likely to experience more pandemics in the future? How can we cultivate readiness and nurture mentoring relationships when face-to-face interactions might be risky?

Far more than ever before, we're using a variety of digital applications and the phone in order to work, promote ideas, learn, shop, conduct transactions, receive health care and other services, pursue our hobbies, socialize, celebrate, and even mourn.

Many of us already have experience building virtual relationships. For example, I have coached the majority of my clients by phone – which has been a well-established practice in the field for years. In my last corporate job, I worked entirely virtually with managers, executives, and team members. I never even met my last manager in person until well after I left the organization. And, we had a great relationship. My husband is now working virtually with his psychotherapy clients. They've adapted and are receiving personal attention. My volunteer work continues as our organization deploys technology to achieve our goals. Virtual relationships like these are happening everywhere around the world, and this practice will increase over time – even beyond COVID-19.

A wealth of online resources is available to network with professionals, identify others with shared passions, and locate experts in fields that intrigue us. We can reach out through LinkedIn and other social media platforms, blogs, forums, websites, texting, and email.

And, as we take online classes or interact virtually for our work, the same dynamic that has brought mentors and mentees together in the past remains alive and well. Leveraging technology, we're getting to know other professionals – engaging, conversing, exchanging information and ideas, questioning, persuading, challenging, offering and receiving guidance, collaborating, inspiring, and creatively solving problems. During these online interactions, we still have rich opportunities to cultivate readiness and nurture mentoring relationships.

Connecting is a perpetual human need that continues in the virtual world.

BIBLIOGRAPHY

Fake Buddha Quotes. Accessed April 1,
    2020. https://fakebuddhaquotes.com/
    when-the-student-is-ready-the-teacher-will-appear/.

Gneiser, Drew. "26 Quotes About Storytelling." Accessed
    February 18, 2020. http://www.drewgneiser.
    com/26-quotes-about-storytelling/.

Good Reads. "Mary Oliver Quotes." Accessed
    February 18, 2020. https://www.goodreads.com/
    quotes/1200218-mysteries-yes-truly-we-live-with-mys-
    teries-too-marvelous-to.

Good Reads. "Readiness Quotes." Accessed April 21, 2020.
    https://www.goodreads.com/quotes/tag/readiness.

McVicker, Laura. "Like Father, Like Son at Local Law
    Firm." *The Columbian,* 2012. Accessed March 8, 2020.
    https://www.columbian.com/news/2012/aug/31/
    brandenburg-law-apprenticeship-Vancouver/.

O'Donnell, B.R.J. "The Odyssey's Millennia-Old Model of
    Mentorship." *The Atlantic.* Accessed February 12, 2020.
    https://www.theatlantic.com/business/archive/2017/10/
    the-odyssey-mentorship/542676/.

University of Cambridge. "What Is Mentoring?" Accessed February 12, 2020. https://www.ppd. admin.cam.ac.uk/professional-development/ mentoring-university-cambridge/what-mentoring.

Webster's New World Dictionary, 3rd College Edition. New York: Simon & Schuster, Inc., 1988.

Wikipedia. "Maria Montessori." Accessed November 18, 2019. https://en.wikipedia.org/wiki/Maria_Montessori.

Wikipedia. "Mentor (*Odyssey*)." Accessed February 12, 2020. https://en.wikipedia.org/wiki/Mentor_(Odyssey).

Wikipedia. "Mentorship." Accessed February 12, 2020. https://en.wikipedia.org/wiki/Mentorship.

Wikipedia. "Moshe Feldenkrais." Accessed January 14, 2020. https://en.wikipedia.org/wiki/Mosh%C3%A9_Feldenkrais.

Wilkie, Rab & David Barry, eds. *Tales of Awakening: Travels, Teachings, and Transcendence with Namgyal Rinpoche (1931 – 2003).* Fairhaven Lantern Media, 2012.

Acknowledgments

This book came to exist through the contributions of many people to whom I am deeply grateful. First of all, I acknowledge my husband and Jungian-oriented psychotherapist, Dr. Gary Seeman. He has known my mentor story for many years and encouraged me to put this story in writing. His idea launched the project. And, his comment in chapter 1 and astute copy edits made it a better book.

Amy Gianesello-Violette, the daughter of my mentor, Fermo Gianesello, responded enthusiastically when I shared the chapter I had written about her dad. Her excitement affirmed the concept for the book.

Chuck Bender, also a Jungian-oriented psychotherapist, helped me create the framework for chapter 1 through his wisdom, insights, and experience as both mentor and mentee. His perspective deepened my understanding of the mentor-mentee relationship.

The nine mentees, who shared their precious stories, generously gave their time for interviews and reviews of drafts. I so much appreciate Issa Abudakar, Bennett Brandenburg, Therese Brooks, Russell Delman, John Greene, Kevin Jordan, Rebecca Keith, and Donna Sinclair for telling their stories and offering their insights about mentoring. Special recognition goes to Liz Williams, who not only shared her story, but also referred me to Russell and Kevin.

My friend, Kay Hudziak, who always comes through with intelligence and enthusiasm, referred me to Bennett.

The other side of the equation – the mentors who appear in the stories – unknowingly also made an indispensable contribution, and some did this posthumously. Without their wisdom and guidance, the mentees' stories would never have materialized.

Richard Bevan, a former colleague, retired organizational change expert, and published author, graciously read my manuscript and provided invaluable insights and observations, which helped shape the book. He also advised me on the publishing process.

Finally, my friends and colleagues who cheered me on throughout the project are too numerous to name. Their support energized me.

About the Author

Janet Birgenheier has been a lifelong learner and communication professional. A graduate of the University of California at Davis with a Bachelor of Arts in English, she briefly worked as a journalist, writing for *The Bridgeport Post* in Connecticut.

After pivoting into corporate America, Janet created communication, training, and change management programs for Electrolux, Dresser Industries (where she met her mentor), Citicorp (now Citigroup), Charles Schwab, Kaiser Permanente, Symantec and for clients of several major consulting firms. She also led her own consulting practice. Late in her career, Janet earned a Master of Science in organization development from the University of San Francisco.

Since retiring from corporate life, she has built and now conducts a career coaching practice, guiding her clients to realize their visions for meaningful work (www.meaningful-work.coach).

The Mentoring Difference: Stories to Inspire Your Career Transformation is Janet's first book.

Made in the USA
Columbia, SC
09 October 2020

22432624R00107